CLOSE!
CLOSE!
CLOSE!

Other books by JOHN FENTON

The A–Z of Industrial Salesmanship
The A–Z of Sales Management
How To Double Your Profits Within the Year
How To Sell Against Competition
Getting Back at the Traffic Warden
101 Ways To Boost Your Business Performance

CLOSE!
CLOSE!
CLOSE!

John Fenton

MERCURY

First published in 1990
by the Mercury Books Division of
W.H. Allen & Co. Plc
Sekforde House, 175–9 St John Street, London EC1V 4LL

Set in Baskerville by Phoenix Photosetting, Chatham
Printed and bound in Great Britain by
Butler & Tanner Ltd, Frome and London

British Library Cataloguing in Publication Data
Fenton, John
    Close! close! close!
    1. Salesmanship
    I. Title
    658.8'5

    ISBN 1–85251–077–3 (hardback)
    ISBN 1–85252–044–2 (paperback)

On 4 December 1987 John Fenton stepped out on to the stage of the Wembley Conference Centre in front of 2,000 British salespeople to present the last – and the greatest – National Sales Convention.

The Convention theme was Close, Close, Close! This is the book of the show.

'. . . nothing happens until somebody *sells* something!'

John Fenton

'It is a glaring glimpse of the obvious to say that no amount of production is of the slightest value unless the products are sold for cash.'

H R H Prince Philip, Duke of Edinburgh

'If you don't *close*, you're working for the competition!'

Alfred Tack

'Almost every buying decision has some negative aspects from the customer's point of view, and these have to be overcome through the use of an appropriate closing technique.'

Heinz M. Goldmann

'You haven't done your job if you quit without asking for the order at least five times.'

J. Douglas Edwards

'In selling, our income and achievement depends almost entirely on our ability to *close*.'

Robin Fielder

In every survey ever conducted asking sales managers what skill they would most like to increase in their salespeople, *closing* has always emerged as the clear winner.

Contents

$$\boxed{1}$$

Can You Succeed in Selling *without* Being a Good Closer?

The short answer is No, you can't.

The long answer begins with why the hell such a dumb question was asked in the first place. And the answer to *that* is because there are so many salespeople out there who can't close, who don't close, who forget to close, who are terrified of closing, who are paranoid about being turned down and won't put themselves in the turn-down-risk situation, who are so negative they expect a 'No' before they even start selling – 'You don't want any more Widgets this month, I suppose, do you?'

This book is for all those dumb salespeople who feel closing is unreal, not for them, not necessary in their business, unethical, high pressure and too complicated.

This book is also for all those professional salespeople who have already recognised that closing is for real, for ever and very necessary, and who want to be even better at it than they are now – and *richer*!

Closing is *not* high pressure. Closing is *not* unethical. If you are being paid to sell and you *don't* close, you are taking money under false pretences. That's stealing! That's fraud! If you are being paid to sell and you don't close, you are working for the competition (we'll explain how and why, later). That's treason!

In this first chapter I am going to convince you, with the aid of logic, facts and statistics, survey results and PROOF, that you cannot survive in selling without closing.

PRESSURE

Let's sympathise with all those thousands of salespeople who think that when you use a closing technique, you are applying *pressure* to the customer.

What is a closing technique? It is anything you can ethically do or say that gets you closer to the decision to buy. For example:

> 'Are you happy with everything?' (Pause, two, three.)
> Customer: 'Er, yyyess, I think so.'
> 'Fine. Can we go ahead, then?' (Shut up.)

This must be about the simplest pair of questions you can ask a customer at the end of a good sales presentation. All doubts are clarified. All questions are answered. A direct 'Will you buy?', then close.

As every salesperson knows, after the second question – 'Can we go ahead, then?' – you *shut up*. And that's when the *pressure* starts.

That's why we said, 'Let's sympathise with all those thousands of salespeople . . .' Because they haven't even got *this* bit right.

Where is the pressure? Think about it. Sure, the pressure is in the silence, but all the customer is doing during those few seconds of silence is mulling things over: 'Should I, shouldn't I? Seems OK. Solves our problem. Can't see any snags. Why not? OK, then.' That's how the customer's mind is working.

So who's sweating? *You*, dummy. The pressure is on *you*, not on the customer. It's unbearable. And after three seconds of that silence you open your stupid fat mouth and ruin the customer's train of thought.

ETHICS

Professional salespeople don't beat up old ladies.

Professional salespeople don't put their feet in the door, seduce the customer's secretary, grab the customer's tie and tighten the knot until they get a 'Yes', knock their competitors, keep selling after they've established that no need exists for their product or service, or after they've established that the customer cannot *afford* to buy.

And professional salespeople don't lie. They don't mislead or misrepresent. They don't exaggerate or give deliberately optimistic delivery dates. They don't promise future delights and rewards that they know will never exist. They don't oversell.

However, strictly in the interest of furthering good customer relations, *all* salespeople are allowed three teeny-weeny white lies . . .

1. 'You're right.'

2. 'It's my fault.'

3. 'It's been a pleasure to meet you.'

THE ONE-IN-FIVE SURVEY

A comprehensive survey conducted by The Institute of Purchasing Management which covered all kinds of people who buy things – purchasing officers, production managers, office managers, directors and the whole range of specifiers – established beyond any doubt that:

ONLY ONE IN FIVE CUSTOMERS WILL EVER VOLUNTEER AN ORDER.

The other four out of five expect, on principle, the salesperson to *ask* for an order. If the salesperson doesn't ask, he or she goes away empty-handed. Believe it. It's true.

So, statistically, those salespeople who *never close*, who never ask for the order, don't even have a chance with 80 per cent of the business that is going. Their market, their *total* market, is an insignificant 20 per cent of the market that good closers can benefit from.

Of course, you never know which of any five customers is the one who *will* volunteer an order. So, the only logical thing to do with this situation is:

NEVER LET A POTENTIAL ORDER GO UNASKED FOR.

THE 8/73 SURVEY

Another piece of international research into both salespeople and their customers which is very relevant to our cause is known as the 8/73 Survey. The main research was conducted to find out how salespeople reacted to *objections* from customers. An objection is a doubt in the customer's mind that is voiced: something they are not sure about, are worried about, are not clear about or don't like about the proposition.

Rarely indeed will a salesperson sail smoothly through a sales presentation, from the opening thirty seconds to the writing-up of the order, without encountering a single objection. Things are simply not that easy.

Objections are like hurdles in a race: you know they're going to be there, you know you've got to get over them, you know what direction you're running in and you know where the finishing-tape is. Your only problem is physical. Can you get over all the hurdles and reach the finishing-tape before you run out of steam? The answer will be a measure of your fitness, your fitness to sell the particular products or services that you have been given responsibility for.

And in the selling profession your fitness is a direct measure of your *knowledge* and how you use it. That knowledge falls into different categories:

Product Knowledge

Application Knowledge

Financial Knowledge

Knowledge of Your Customer's Business

Knowledge of Your Customer's Markets

Knowledge of Your Competitors

Knowledge of Selling Techniques

Many customers are not very forthcoming about voicing their doubts, but they need to be encouraged. Otherwise they bottle them up and the salesperson, when closing time arrives, gets a 'No' in response to the first attempt to ask for the order. And many salespeople, faced with this 'No' mentally breathe a big sigh of relief and escape as fast as possible, convincing themselves that they've done the best they can.

WRONG, WRONG, WRONG!

Nine times out of ten that '*No*' wasn't a real 'No'; it was the customer's way of saying, 'I'm not quite sure, yet.' And a 'No, not yet' is very, very different from a 'No, not ever.'

This is the simplest way to deal with that first 'No'.

'Ah. Is there something you're still not sure about, then?' (Pause, two, three.)

The customer starts telling you the doubt. Listen, deal with it, then ask for the order again.

'Are you happy with everything, now? Can we go ahead, then?'

Any more doubts will come out straight away and can be dealt with following the same pattern. Close again. Hurdles, Hurdles, Hurdles!

Back to the 8/73 Survey. For the purpose of presenting the figures, all 'Nos' are classified as 'No, not yets': that is, objections based on a doubt. Research into the reaction of salespeople to the objections they received from their customers revealed:

44 per cent gave up after receiving the *first* objection

22 per cent gave up after receiving the *second* objection

16 per cent gave up after receiving the *third* objection

10 per cent gave up after receiving the *fourth* objection

So, 92 per cent gave up after *four* objections, leaving only 8 per cent of the salespeople still selling. That's the 8 part of the 8/73 Survey.

The 73 part comes from the second half of the research, which concentrated on the customers in order to establish the kind and the quantity of objections they voiced when faced with the salespeople they'd been dealing with.

The kind of objections pinpointed are not relevant here, but the quantity is. The research established without any doubt that 73 per cent of customers voiced *five or more* objections before being sure enough to place an order.

So there you have it. These two parts of the one survey prove that 8 per cent of salespeople will win 73 per cent of the business that's going.

In fact, the situation is significantly *worse* than this, because both the 92 per cent of salespeople who gave up and the 8 per cent still going after four objections are the salespeople who actually got as far as asking for the order *at least once*. The salespeople who don't *close* at all aren't even in the race.

THE BEST CLOSERS

Now I'm going to hit you where it *really* hurts. Smack in your ego!

Who are the *best* closers? Who are the people who *never* give up, who *never* take no for an answer? Answer: children between the ages of six and nine.

Maybe it's happened to you. Maybe you've seen it happen to some other parent. Visualise a sunny Sunday morning in the park, just before lunch.

'Dad, can I have an ice cream?'

'No. It's too near your lunchtime.'

'Oh, go on, Dad. Just a little one.'

'*No*. I've told you.'

'Oh, please, Dad. I *want* one.'

'*No*. That's enough.'

(Tears and fifty more decibels.) 'I wannaa iiicce creeeeeamm.'

'Oh, f'Christ's sake. *All right*. But don't tell your mother.'

The little horrors *never* give up. Why is that? It's because before the age of nine their conditioning hasn't taken effect. Think about it. All through your life, through your early childhood, through school, through early adulthood and your first tastes of commerce

WHATEVER YOU WANTED TO DO, SOMEONE, SOMEWHERE, ALWAYS SAID '*NO*'!

We are all thoroughly conditioned to *expect* 'No'. Is it therefore any wonder that it's always been so difficult getting to grips with closing a sale? We are trying to change the world.

Apart from taking note of the techniques which I'm going to teach you so that you become a *great* closer (these will be covered in depth later in the book), all you have to do is change your normal in-built 'No' expectation into a 'Yes' expectation, just like that horrible child in the park. Every time you feel yourself beginning to chicken out towards the end of a sales presentation, just remember that kids aged six to nine are much better at it than you. Then let your ego take over. How much has your education and training cost since *you* were that good? What a *waste*!

Remember, too, your greatest ally: the bumble bee. Aerodynamically, it is *impossible* for the bumble bee to fly – that huge, heavy, hairy body; those tiny wings.

BUT NOBODY EVER *TOLD* THE BUMBLE BEE!

One final thing to remember for when you're feeling timid about closing a sale:

NO ONE HAS EVER BEEN STRUCK BY LIGHTNING FOR ASKING FOR AN ORDER.

There is not one recorded fatality in respect of closing the sale. It is one of the *safest* things on God's Earth.

Can you succeed in selling *without* being a good closer? No, you can't. So remember Sir Brian Rix's first and most famous film, *Reluctant Heroes* – what a perfect name for novice salespeople! Remember the catch phrase that Sergeant Ronald Shiner hammered into rookie Private Rix:

I CAN, I MUST, AND I WILL.

That you *can* is not in doubt, is it? It is not a physical impossibility for you to open your mouth and ask for an order.

That you *must* is demonstrated by the results of the two pieces of research we've just discussed: the One-in-Five Survey and the 8/73 Survey. Are you a dummy or an intelligent human being?

That you *will* is dependent on how well your ego, your pride and your self-esteem combine to overcome your conditioning and make you *want* to be better than kids of six to nine in the job you've been trained for and are paid to do.

2

For Sales Managers and Sales Directors Only . . . on Excuses and Autopsy Check Lists

(Salespeople should move directly to Chapter 3)

I want to put a question to all the sales managers and sales directors who are reading this book. Have you ever analysed the call reports you receive from your salespeople over, say, a six-month period to pinpoint the kind of *excuses* they give for not coming away with an order? Note, *'excuses'*, not reasons!

At Structured Training Ltd we've done this many times for many clients. As a result, and without breaking any confidences, we can present our own universal UK Top Ten Excuses for *not* closing.

1. The customer wants to think it over for a few days.

2. The customer wants to wait till the other quotations have been received.

3. The customer doesn't want to spend that kind of money.

4. The customer wants more discount than we can give him/her.

5. The customer wants to stick to his/her normal supplier.

6. The customer needs it by next week and we can't deliver for four weeks.

7. The customer doesn't think enough of his/her customers will buy it.

8. The customer feels it is too much trouble to change over.

9. The customer feels it is too complicated for his/her people.

10. The customer was too busy to listen properly.

Any of these ten strike chords? Any bring back memories of last week or last month?

There are many ways to eliminate, or at least minimise, these kinds of excuses for not closing, but more on this later. First let us dwell on three more things that will stop you getting the order, three that you will *never* in a million years see on *any* salesperson's call report. These are our Top Three Reasons (not excuses) for *losing* the order.

1. I loused up the demonstration.

2. I got up the customer's nose by:
    arriving twenty minutes late;
    not having the right spec. sheet;
    smoking in the office;
    smelling like a brewery;
    wearing my colour co-ordinates – red tie, red socks, red belt and
        red-framed spectacles!

And the reason that eclipses *all* the other twelve rolled into one:

3. I DIDN'T ASK FOR THE ORDER.

I will deal with the Top Three Reasons comprehensively later in the book. To eliminate *your* version of the Top Ten Excuses, all you need are some Autopsy Check Lists (ACLs).

Every time you get an excuse on a salesperson's call report, hand him or her the appropriate ACL and get it filled in. It's a form of remedial training and people soon catch on. Doing the job right in the first place is much easier than having to complete the ACL later.

Opposite is a sample ACL.

Autopsy Check List

EXCUSE: The customer wants to think it over for a few days.

Why does he/she want to think it over?

What specifically does he/she want to think over?

How many specific doubts does he/she still have?

Why is he/she still suffering from *any* doubts after you've given him/her your full presentation?

What proofs can you give him/her to clear up further any doubts?

How many of these proofs did you use during your presentation?

Did you actually *ask* for the order?

How many times?

How did you *ask*? What were the precise words you used?

When are you going back to see him/her?

Write out below IN DETAIL what you are going to say to him/her that will give you the best chance of winning the order.

Have this ACL completed and on my desk by 3.00 p.m. tomorrow.

General Sales Manager

$$\boxed{3}$$

How to Help Customers
Make up their Mind

There are many different reasons why customers will say 'Yes' to a deal. In his book *The Super Salesman's Handbook*, William Davis lists a number of them, and I would like to elaborate on some of his points.

1. They want to own what you have to offer.

This is the easiest close. You have a desirable product and have managed to convince the customer of that fact.

2. They think it will benefit their company.

Again, you have done a good job. You have demonstrated the benefits of the product, proving the existence of a favourable cost/benefit ratio.

3. They fear that if they don't buy now, they will have to pay more later on.

You have successfully generated a sense of urgency by worrying the customer about the risk of a price increase next month.

4. They can't resist the word 'New'.

New has always been the best word to use in selling. Even today it still works magic. Telling a customer that you have a *new* brochure or a *new* product will often open doors which would never open for yet another meeting about the same *old* product.

5. They like spending money.

This is not often the case, but don't ever underestimate that old chestnut about keeping up with the Joneses. Some people are determined to *beat* the Joneses. And sometimes at the very top end of a luxury market prospective customers may like to think they are 'pampering themselves' with your product – a crate of champagne, perhaps, a Rolls-Royce, or an indoor swimming-pool.

6. They like you.

Most really successful salespeople are likeable personalities, although as not everyone likes the same sort of people, no one can rely on just a winning smile to get them through every time.

7. They are not happy with their present suppliers and want to change.

You may simply have arrived at the right place at the right time with the right deal. Or the customer might have contacted you. Whichever, your assurances are going to be of paramount importance. Break one promise and you're *dead*.

8. They are in a hurry.

If this is the case, it is another lucky break for you, and not one which can be planned for. Find out why, and offer absolutely *no* discount.

9. They think it will make them look good.

Peer-group motivation is very important to all of us. If you can convince the prospective customers that their chairman and fellow directors will be very impressed by the savings they will make by going for your product, or by the terms of the deal you are offering, they will be more likely to buy.

10. They want to take advantage of discounts.

It's all a question of how you present the deal. Just don't *start* with the discount. That's not selling; it's giving money away.

11. They like making bold decisions.

If you're up against the dominant buyer, who is as cocky as they come, positive and loves innovation, maybe this time it is *you* who should display caution. But only to the extent of working out *his or her* cost/benefit ratio twice, just to be sure.

12. They have heard that a rival has done well with your product or service.

The use of referrals and word of mouth can never be beaten. It means that the salesperson comes to the meeting with an advantage since the prospective customer is already keen to buy. If the sale falls through, the salesperson should seriously consider following an alternative career.

13. They don't have the courage to say 'No'.

But *don't* oversell or overstock. All you'll get later on is put-offs; you'll never get face to face again. The customer won't risk it.

14. They are greedy.

And the sales person has been able to stimulate this greed by painting pictures of future profits or ways to cut out a rival.

15. They feel insecure.

And the salesperson has a strong case for added security.

16. They need, or think they need, your product or services.

If they have already identified a need, you simply have to convince them that *yours* is the right product for them.

17. They are drunk/happy/in the right mood.

Lucky you! But remember, luck isn't an abstract; it's a place: the place where preparation meets opportunity.

18.   They are afraid that someone else will beat them to it.

The Joneses again! This could be a fear which the salesperson has planted in their minds, or it could be there already and simply needs exploiting.

WHY PEOPLE SAY 'NO'

It's not *all* going to come up smelling of roses. William Davis also has a list of reasons why people say 'No'.

1.   They haven't been listening.

One of our Top Ten Excuses for not closing, remember? It may or may not be the fault of the salesperson, but there is nothing to suggest that the customer won't listen next time if they are caught at a better moment.

2.   They only wanted to find out if you had any good ideas.

Or to check prices. If you do have some good ideas, then there is still an opportunity to follow up on whatever initial impression you have made. If you don't have any good ideas, you had better sit down with a pad and pencil and *think* of some.

3.   They are prejudiced against your product.

Find out why. Is it misinformation or bad past experience? Whichever, you have an opportunity to change their opinions with information, with explanation and especially with referrals from other satisfied customers.

4.   They don't like you.

This could be a problem and if you can't crack it, it might be better to suggest that someone else on the team tries to follow up next time. If that someone else gets the *same* reaction, chances are it's the customer, not you.

5. They hate making decisions.

Then the salesperson will need to look for opportunities to *help* them make decisions.

6. They don't have the authority to make decisions.

Then the salesperson knows he or she has the wrong person and can find out who the right one is before making another approach.

7. They haven't got the money.

There might be ways round that if the problem is looked at closely enough: for example, stage payments, HP, leasing.

8. They are afraid of the consequences of saying 'Yes'.

In this case it is up to the salesperson to allay their fears, even if it takes several visits, demonstrations at other customers' premises, guarantees, personal assurances and, of course, a dozen third-party reference letters.

9. They are tired/drunk/in the wrong mood.

Again, this is just bad timing and another call on another day could easily produce an order. Prospective customers will presumably appreciate the salesperson's sensitivity in leaving them alone when they don't feel like talking.

10. They don't like change.

If this is the case, they need to become accustomed to the idea of what the product or service will do for them, until they feel comfortable with it. Resistance to change is fear of the unknown, of stepping out of the frying-pan into the fire. And often it is based on lethargy: it's too much trouble to change. Many businesses go broke every year due to this kind of lethargy.

11. They haven't understood your presentation.

Have you been talking in jargon? Regular open-ended questions will show up this problem and then the salesperson can put it right.

12. They are misers.

If so, they need to be shown how much money they will save or make by investing in the product.

13. They are simply not convinced.

Then the salesperson needs to produce more evidence.

14. They know someone who will make a better offer.

The salesperson needs to show enough interest to find out who this person is and, if possible, what the offer is. If he or she can't top it, at least something will have been learned about what the competition is up to.

15. They hope you will come back and improve your terms.

This is tactics. After all, it *is* their job to get the best possible deal. You should certainly try again, provided it doesn't mean giving away too much.

16. They don't like the colour/shape/feel of your product.

This doesn't sound like the *real* reason. Explore. Perhaps whatever they dislike can be changed or they can be convinced that the benefits outweigh the problems.

17. They are worried about your after-sales service.

By demonstrating the degree of service which you are willing to put in and by proving that you have actually done so in the past, you will be able to build up their confidence in the company as a whole. The salesperson needs to show that he or she is willing to take 'personal' responsibility for the customer's account and doesn't think the job ends with the close.

18. Their wives/husbands won't let them say 'Yes'.

Then the salesperson probably needs to meet that wife/husband in order to convince them as well.

NEW TO THE JOB

Job changes within companies that are potential customers often present good opportunities for closing sales. First there are the outgoing incumbents of jobs. They no longer have to worry about getting into trouble for making decisions that might be somewhat against current company policy or a significant change in the traditional way of doing things. By the time the consequences of their actions are known, they will be safely out of the way. If they like the salesperson, therefore, and have been procrastinating about making a decision because of cautiousness, this might be the time to turn them round.

Newcomers to jobs, however, are an even better bet. Whether they are newly recruited or newly promoted, executives coming into a decision-making role are always anxious to make their mark. They are receptive to any ideas which will make them look good, and their superiors are usually happy to let them get on with the job for the first few months. A newly promoted or appointed executive also gives the salesperson the opportunity to resurrect proposals that were rejected by a predecessor and to re-present them.

CHOOSING YOUR WORDS

The words which a salesperson uses during the closing part of his or her presentation, and indeed all the way through it, can determine whether a 'Yes' or 'No' response is forthcoming.

Some words are good for closing and others are bad. Rather than ask someone to *pay* for your product, for instance, you should ask them to *invest* in it. By simply changing one word you are immediately showing them that to say 'Yes' would be a sensible move, that it would *make* not *cost* money, and you are arming them with words to use when justifying their decision to peers or superiors.

Instead of asking them to *sign* a form, ask them to *OK* it. We all have an in-built fear of putting our names to things, particularly if there is small print involved, just in case we are signing away our lives. If we are asked to OK something, however, the other party is recognising that we have a certain status and is asking us to be agreeable and helpful, which most of us are happy to be.

I have talked already about the power of the word 'New', but it cannot be overstressed. Architects, for instance, are notorious for disliking salespeople, but they love innovation. So if you ring up and tell them you have a 'new design manual' and you would like to give them their copy, you will be in. If you are displaying a new product at an exhibition and you hang a large sign over the product with just that one word on it, you will immediately attract a crowd. If you are arranging an appointment by phone with a potentially hostile firm, emphasise the 'new' angle and you will be in. A surprising number of companies fail to capitalise on this simple fact.

When talking to a prospective customer avoid vague words and phrases like *I wonder if* and replace them with *I'm sure that*. All customers like to feel that the seller is confident of his or her subject and product. If you show any doubts or hesitancy they will be less willing to take a risk on your recommendation.

Try talking about *savings* rather than *costs*. The differences are obvious and there are often ways of reversing the two terms in a presentation.

The Possessive Technique

Try to make customers feel that the product is *theirs* as early in the sale as you can. This is achieved by using words like *you* and *your* as often as possible: 'When *you* have been using *your* Universal Widget Crusher for a few weeks, *you'll* be amazed at how much *your* crushing costs have been reduced.'

The Five Words That Really Turn Customers On

Research has shown that there are five words which always make customers sit up, listen and *remember* after the salesperson has left.

They are:

Increase

Improve

Reduce

Save

Gain

The more they are used – *all* of them – the better, both throughout the presentation and throughout the closes.

4

How Many Closing Techniques Do You Need to Master?

To be a brilliant closer of sales, how many closing techniques do you need to have mastered, to have in your bag, ready to use when the opportunity presents itself?

When we were preparing the material for the 1987 National Sales Convention, one of the things we did was to research and document as many different closing techniques as we could find. We were still going strong when we got to 165! We stopped there because we had only half a day for the Convention.

So how many of these 165 should you seek to master? The answer is six -- that's all. Whether a salesperson is selling high tech to industry or to specifiers like architects, or is selling staples – fmcg (fast-moving consumer goods) or consumer durables to retailers, or products for resale to supermarkets and pubs – the number of closing techniques required to be a master closer is just *six*.

Again, it was research that proved this: a survey of 100 very successful high-tech salespeople and 100 very successful staple salespeople which set out to establish their *favourite* closes.

HIGH-TECH FAVOURITE CLOSES

74 per cent of high-tech salespeople favour the Alternative Choice Close. For example:

'Do you want us to do the commissioning or will your technical people do it?'

'Do you need single-phase or three-phase power supply?'
'Do you prefer the white finish or the satin aluminium?'
'Will you be paying cash or should we send an invoice?'
'Shall we deliver or will you collect?'
'Do you want delivery on Tuesdays or Thursdays?'
'I'm in your area next Tuesday. Shall I come and see you in the morning or the afternoon?'

9 per cent of the same sample of high-tech salespeople preferred the Concession Close. For example:
'If we can get you delivery a week earlier than normal, can I have your order today?'
'If I can persuade production to paint it your house colour, do we have a deal?'
'If I can shave another 2·5 per cent off the price, can we go ahead?'

7 per cent of high-tech salespeople, however, preferred the Summary Close, which is a particularly good weapon for overcoming the 'I want to think it over' objection. For example:
'Let's just recap on the things we've covered today in our proposals. We've covered the performance of the equipment, and I think you said that you and everyone else was more than happy on this point. Am I correct?'
'Yes.'
'We've covered the question of acceptability to your workforce, and again everyone is happy that the demonstrations were well received and that our operator-training programme will cover all eventualities. Yes?'
'Yes.'
'We've covered the running costs, and I think you agree that they are lower than any of the alternative solutions you've been considering . . .' (raise eyebrows at customer)
'Yes.'
'And we've covered the maintenance costs and after-sales-service aspects to your total satisfaction, have we not?'
'Yes.'
'In fact, the cost/benefit analysis for the equipment shows you get

total payback inside a year – well within your budget. Have I covered everything?'

'I think so.'

'OK. Can we go ahead, then? Can you get me an order number so that I can get things moving today?'

4 per cent of the high-tech salespeople in the survey preferred to use a Fear Close (which doesn't mean threatening to send the boys round the next day if an order is not forthcoming). Normally this means fear of future price rises. For example:

'We expect a 9 per cent price increase next month, and the way exchange rates are moving, I wouldn't be surprised if this puts prices up another 6 per cent. I can hold the price we've quoted until the end of this month, I think, but to be absolutely certain, it would be safer to push the green button today. How about it?'

Or:

'What would happen if you had a fire *before* you'd installed all these replacement extinguishers? Tonight, for example? If you decide now, they'll be here this afternoon. Why tempt fate when we're this close?'

3 per cent of the high-tech salespeople voted for the Verbal Proof Story Close:

'I can understand your wanting to spend some time thinking this over, Mr Smith. In fact, I had a very similar situation some months ago over at Universal Widgets. They had been using Snook's Oils for years and it took their works manager a long time to decide to switch to us. But since they did, their oil stocks have reduced by a third because of our twenty-four hour delivery service. They've got a much better tool life all round through using our special cutting oils and they reckon that overall they're saving about £2,400 a week. Look (produces third-party reference letter), this is what UW's works manager said in a letter to us only last month. Would it help you to decide if I had a word with UW and took you over to talk to your opposite number there? Every week you think about it could be costing your company the same kind of money – £2,400 a week.

That's nearly £125,000 a year! Or can we get something started today?'

Here we have good, true, relevant story, with figures, about some-one with whom your prospective customer can identify. It's followed up with an offer to set up a meeting, then reinforced with talk of the kind of money being lost while the customer thinks about it and doesn't act. The finale is an Alternative Choice Close: the meeting or give me the order now!

This is the winning combination for Verbal Proof closing. The chances are that the prospective customer will not take up the offer of a meeting but will be satisfied with the letter and the fact that you were confident enough to offer the meeting.

So, five different techniques received 97 per cent of the votes in the survey.

Alternative Choice

Concession

Summary

Fear

Verbal Proof

If you add one more, you probably have the best six going, and that sixth technique is simply:

Come out and ask for the order

The best way is to use the One-Two Close:

'Are you happy with everything?'
'Er, yyyess, I think so.'
'Fine. Can we go ahead, then?'

And then, *shut up!*

STAPLE FAVOURITE CLOSES

The bulk of sales to retailers is of fast-moving consumer goods and consumer durables. Called 'staple' selling, it calls for a very different art to high-tech selling.

In this sector of the survey, 64 per cent of salespeople nominated the Order Form Close as their preferred method. This is the nearest thing to an automatic close that any retail salesperson can get. It means having the order form out and ready in the clipboard from the moment you enter the store. It also means having a copy of last month's order on the left-hand side of the clipboard and the entire range of products printed on the order form.

The salesperson starts by checking what is in the store's stockroom and then goes to the shelves where his or her company's products are on display. This means that the amount of stock sold since the last visit and the amount left to sell are known quantities. With retailing moving at the speed it does these days, overselling is one of the worst mistakes any salesperson can make.

The salesperson then talks to the store manager and suggests they walk around the store together. While they are doing this (and most managers will agree unless they are particularly busy), the salesperson refers to his or her order forms and to the goods on display, asking questions as they go along.

'How's the new line moving? Is it as good as I said it would be? Great! Same again this month, or would you like to increase it to six cases?'

'Is this line still slow? It's going to pick up, don't worry. We've got an advertising campaign starting next week. It would be a good idea to fill the shelf in preparation. Shall I put you down for two cases?'

'We've got a special offer this month on this line. It will be making a big splash over the next few weeks. Do you think four cases would be enough?'

When the salesperson has been through every relevant line on the order form, plus any new lines which have not previously been discussed with the manager, he or she makes a final check on the form, turns it round to the manager and says:

'Fine, I think we've covered everything. Would you just OK this for me as usual, here at the bottom?'

The next favourite, with 16 per cent, is the Alternative Choice Close.

'Would you like six cases or eight?'

'Shall we deliver it all this week or would you rather take some of it next week?'

The Summary Close received 8 per cent of the vote, the Fear Close 6 per cent and the Concession Close 4 per cent.

That makes 98 per cent across just five different closes. If you add on the 'Just come out and ask for the order' Close, you have covered most eventualities and styles.

Remember what I said in Chapter 1:

NO ONE HAS EVER BEEN STRUCK BY LIGHTNING FOR ASKING FOR AN ORDER.

CLOSING A SALE HAS NEVER CAUSED A FATALITY.

IT IS ONE OF THE SAFEST PASTIMES IN THE WORLD.

Remember also the ABC of selling:

ALWAYS BE CLOSING.

TWO ADDITIONAL KEY CLOSING TOOLS

1. The Most Powerful Question in Selling

This is a question which you can ask at the beginning of each sale in a number of different ways.

Let's assume that you have done some research and found that a particular company uses widgets, but you haven't been able to establish any more tangible objective than wanting to sell this company some of your widgets. You make contact with their key decision maker, preferably face to face, but by telephone will do, and you say:

'Good morning, Mr Jones. As I understand it, your company uses a lot of widgets.' (Pause.) 'My company sells widgets. Very good ones. I'd like to see you using some of ours. Please may I ask you a very direct question?' (Here it comes.)

'What do I need to do to get you to buy some of your widgets from us?'

There are some variations on the same theme, such as:

'What do we need to do to get on your list of approved suppliers?'

Then, whatever is suggested, you can add in some confirmation and commitment before you actually do it:

'Fair enough. If we can do that, will you place some of your business our way?'

As you become more proficient at competitive selling, you will find that those three words – 'if we can' – will unlock more doors than you ever thought possible.

You could also attempt to quantify the business:

'How much of your business would you be able to move to us?'

'How soon?'

'What sizes?'

Then, provided you do what is suggested, to the manager's complete satisfaction, the business will be yours.

2. Starting with a Close

Why waste time on a long sales talk if you can close the sale immediately? Obviously you have to start with a few preliminaries, such as 'How do you do' and 'My name is John Fenton', but you could then go straight into the Suppose Test Close:

'Suppose you like me . . . Suppose you like the product . . . Suppose the price is acceptable . . . Suppose you like everything . . . Are you ready to buy today?'

If the answer is 'Yes' or 'I could be', then you know that you have a serious prospect and you can go for it with all cylinders firing. If the answer is 'No' or 'I doubt it', you've got some more work to do in order to bring your prospective customer to the 'ready' state. That could be easy or it could be hard.

Now read on . . .

5

Making Sure the Customer is *Ready* to be Closed

Successful closing is not just something that ends a sale. It cannot be separated out from successful selling.

In order to maximise the chances of receiving a 'Yes' and minimise the chances of a 'No', you need to create an environment which is conducive to a successful close. This means that from the moment you come into contact with the customer you must start setting the mood. You don't necessarily have to ask for the order the moment you walk in the door, but you do have to start 'conditioning' the customer to say 'Yes' from the word go. You both need to be thinking that a close is likely all the way through the presentation.

There is a principle, called the Six P Principle, to follow here.

PROPER PLANNING PREVENTS
POSSIBLE POOR PERFORMANCE

You need two basic plans. First, the *strategy*. This is the medium-to long-term plan for how to achieve the overall objectives. Strategy is about *tomorrow*. What are the objectives with this customer in developing the account? Second, the *tactics*. This is the short-term plan for how to achieve each specific objective. Tactics are about *today*.

Many salespeople can see the wood and the trees (strategy and tactics) individually but fail to see both together. Both plans must be flexible, since they need to be able to grow with the customer. They need to be organic.

DON'T MAKE ASSUMPTIONS

A common mistake in these early stages is to make assumptions. This is very dangerous. Too many salespeople assume, for instance, that they don't have to plan in order to close.

Some assume that because a customer has agreed to see them, they are automatically going to make a sale, so the salesperson goes in in a relaxed state of mind, not selling themselves, their company or their products. They are then often amazed to find themselves leaving without the order.

Others assume that the customer likes the competition better than them. This defeatist attitude means they are beaten before they start. It is seldom based on any rational thinking and is just a gut-felt inferiority complex.

Some assume that the buying decision can't be made today, so they leave without asking. What evidence do they have for assuming that?

Others assume that the customer has all the information needed for making a buying decision, and consequently don't check for understanding.

If you assume that a sale is not possible, the chances are that the customer will assume the same. Equally, the reverse is true.

The word 'assume' breaks down very symbolically into three:

ASS   U   ME

If you assume, it is an even bet that you're going to make an ASS out of somebody . . . and it's an odds-on bet that it's going to be YOU.

There are some assumptions, however, that you *should* go in with:

Today *is* the day.

You *do* offer the best value-for-money package.

You *do* stand by everything you say.

[52]

If you demonstrate your complete belief in everything that you are saying, the customer will believe you. Inexperienced salespeople sometimes appear surprised when the customer says 'Yes'. This is because they had assumed they would get a 'No'. It should be the other way round, and once it is, the whole emphasis of the meeting will alter.

GETTING TO THE RIGHT PERSON

To ensure that you are talking to the right person, research is vital. There is nothing worse than getting to the end of a long presentation only to hear:
'I'll talk to my boss.'
Or:
'I'll put it forward at the next budget meeting.'
Or:
'The person you should be talking to is in the States at the moment, but if you would like to come back in a month or so . . .'
The first thing to do is identify the MAN. This is all about researching the customer's ability to say 'Yes'.

M   Money: Can they afford the product?
A   Authority: Can this person authorise the purchase?
N   Need: Do they need/want the product?

If you get the MAN identification right early in the sales call, your chances of successfully closing increase dramatically. The best way of identifying the MAN is simply by *asking*.
'So that I don't waste any of your time, are you the right person to talk to for this sort of decision?'
You can do this at the first visit, but be careful, because customers might lie, not wanting to admit that they are not in authority. So you must give their egos room to breathe. Try putting it another way.

'Is there anyone else you would like to involve in our discussions?'
Or:
'Is there anybody else you would like me to invite to the demonstration we are going to mount for you?'
Or:
'Should I send a copy of the figures to anybody else?'
As a general rule, always try to involve the boss.

On the road to closing a sale you will come across various people.

The Decision Influencers

These are the people who make recommendations but do not actually make the final decisions. They have to be courted. They have to be convinced the product will benefit themselves and their departments and they have to be given a reason to lobby on your behalf. They are susceptible to flattery and should be told how important they are to the decision and how much their input counts.

The Decision Maker

The decision maker is probably the decision influencer's boss and is, as the name suggests, the one who makes the decisions. If you can get to him or her direct, then go for it. Don't, however, ignore the influencers. You might want to go back later with another proposition and it would be difficult if you were to find them antagonistic towards you, blocking your way to the decision maker. If they feel you have slighted them, they will take every opportunity to bad-mouth your product or service once it is installed and will ensure that you get no repeat orders.

If the influencer agrees to recommend your solution but the decision maker is unavailable, you need to use the Subject To Close. For example:

'I understand that Mr Smith isn't available today, but just to clarify it in my mind, subject to his approval, are you ready to proceed?'

When Mr Smith returns the following week, you can use this agreement to pre-close the sale.

[54]

'I was with your colleague last week, tying up the loose ends, and he did say to me that, subject to your final approval, he was perfectly happy with the situation.'

In this way you have made the influencer commit himself. He will lose face if he consequently fails to get the solution accepted and you have an impressive third-party reference to use in the meeting with the boss.

Decision-making Unit

When purchasing responsibility is spread over several departments, or involves a number of different people, it is known as a decision-making unit. If this is the case, the salesperson must find out exactly how the unit is constructed. Who has responsibility for which part? Who reports to whom? How does the unit interrelate with the whole company? Does one member have the final decision or veto? What timescales and communication methods are used?

To answer these questions the salesperson will have to instigate some detailed research and undertake some perceptive questioning. This is not easy, but it *is* very necessary.

The rest of this chapter is a compendium of rules and techniques that will help you bring your customer to that essential 'ready' state.

ENSURE COMPLETE UNDERSTANDING

Never try to baffle prospective customers with technical jargon, or any language which they won't understand. They probably won't be impressed, and they certainly won't make a buying decision unless they are sure they have fully grasped what you are saying.

They may not want to admit that they don't understand, so it is up to you to check that they do. If they don't fully understand the proposal and don't want to admit to the fact, they will not close. They will say something along the lines of:

'Fine, well, leave me some literature and I'll give you a call.'

Remember, you can't close until the prospective customer *completely understands* your proposal, so *check understanding at each stage*.

If You Don't Close, You Are Working For The Competition

If you do all the preliminary work of identifying prospective customers, approaching them, alerting them to their problems and explaining ways in which these can be solved, but you then fail to close the sale, you have done nothing but set that customer up to buy from the next person who comes asking for the order, and that will be your competitor.

STRUCTURED TRAINING'S STEPS OF THE SALE

Closing must be a pre-planned part of the overall sale, an end which you are working methodically towards right from the first moment of contact.

To make a sale, salespeople must create a need to buy within the prospective customer which equals their own need to sell. That can be achieved in stages throughout the sales process. By breaking the process down into its constituent parts, you can identify each stage's objectives and ensure that they are achieved before moving on. You can also measure your performance by generating success ratios for each stage and comparing one month or one quarter with the next, to ensure performance is consistently improving.

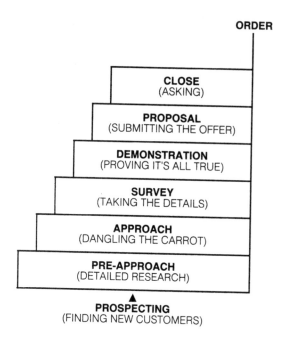

THE JAPANESE WAY

One Japanese computer company (FACOM) produces a sales check list which has made them a winner in every market they tackle. They call it 'Profile of a Sale' and it lists the eleven key stages a salesperson is required to go through, from the beginning to the end of a potential sale. (See page 58.)

AIM TO ACHIEVE A WIN-WIN SITUATION

The win-win situation means that the seller wins by selling and the buyer wins by buying. If you give your customer room to win, then he or she will buy from you again. If a sale seems like a victory to the seller at the expense of the buyer, it is an unsatisfactory close, even though the sale was made.

If customers are unsure about making the final decision, it means

Profile of a Sale

1 RESEARCH PROSPECTIVE CUSTOMER
   Annual report. Company structure. Cross directorships.

2 ESTABLISH CONTACTS
   Plan objectives for each call. Top down or bottom up?

3 MEET DECISION MAKER AND RECOMMENDER

4 ESTABLISH NEEDS AND WANTS WITH DECISION
   MAKER
   Probe for company five-year plans with decision maker.
   What are the company's key business decisions?
   Who makes these decisions?

5 BASIS OF DECISION
   Unique to FACOM?
   Relevant to decision maker. Written down?
   Can FACOM satisfy all points?
   Favourable cost/benefit ratio?

6 FACOM REVIEW
   Review Basis of Decision with manager and assess
   percentage chance of obtaining the order.

7 RESOURCE ALLOCATION FOR SURVEY

8 SURVEY
   Review findings with customer's middle management.
   Have you established all objections?

9 PRESENTATION
   Plan and rehearse.

10 PROPOSAL
   Document only what you have sold.
   Does it satisfy all the points in the Basis of Decision?
   Sense of urgency?

11 CLOSE
   Close quickly or find out why not.
   Have you followed the Profile?

that they are afraid of something. In most cases this is a fear engendered by lack of knowledge. They need to be *made brave enough* to make the decision. That means they need to be reassured and helped over the fear of change.

WATCH FOR THE 'READY' SIGNALS

Timing is vital in closing any sale. How do you decide the right moment to ask for the order? If you get the timing right, your chances of receiving a positive response go up by over 50 per cent.

To help you decide on the right moment, look for 'ready' signals. This might be something buyers say or do which reveals that they are ready. A typical verbal 'ready' signal might be:

'Do you offer the system in other configurations?'

The physical, non-verbal 'ready' signals might be harder to catch and require a reasonable knowledge of body language. Don't rely on just one body gesture but look for clusters of posture changes which

demonstrate that the customer's resistance is disappearing and he or she is feeling relaxed and open towards you and your suggestions.

On the preceding page a salesperson is selling to a customer who is seated behind his desk. The salesperson is painting pictures and emphasising key points with his hands. He seeks to transmit his enthusiasm for what he is selling to the customer. Such enthusiasm is infectious. (In fact, in selling there is only one thing *more* infectious and that is *LACK* of enthusiasm.) The customer's fingers are pressed together at the tips, in a pyramid. This tells the salesperson that his proposals are being critically appraised but there are still some doubts. The customer is leaning back in his chair. If he were to change his position, stop pyramiding with his hands and lean forward towards the salesperson, he would be indicating that his appraisal was finished and he was ready. If, on the other hand, his pyramiding were to change to folded arms across his chest and he remained leaning *back* in his chair, the body language signal would be negative. He would probably, but not definitely, have decided 'No'.

Above are three different reactions of a senior executive listening to a sales presentation. On the left he is pyramiding again, which

means critical appraisal. A sure 'ready' signal is when his fingers entwine and his hands comfortably clasp his lower stomach, arms at rest, as in the centre. He has decided. Ask the right closing question and he will uncross his legs and lean forward, as on the right. He is ready to *buy*.

Here are three stages of positive evaluation. On the left the customer, seated behind his desk, is doubtful. His doubt is signified by the hand which strokes his chin and by the arm that is defensively guarding his chest. He is leaning back. As the salesperson talks, something hits a hot button. The customer stops stroking his chin. His head tilts to one side, resting on a vertical finger and on the hand that was stroking his chin. He still leans back and he still presents the defensive arm barrier, but he is interested. If the salesperson sees that he or she has hit the hot button and runs with it, the customer's interest may build. He may lean forward, chin still held in his hand, one elbow on the desk. His defensive arm barrier drops to the surface of the desk. *Ready*, steady, go for it.

Here, on the left, is a very uninterested, unresponsive junior decision influencer. He sees changes and that means more work for him if he goes along with the salesperson's proposals. He is limp. There are no tangible defensive barriers, but anyone can see that he is negative.

How can the salesperson stimulate him into positive action? Perhaps play on the kudos of having brought about a significant technological improvement for his company, something that outweighs the hassle of extra work? A hot button again, and this time we know the signal is green because the leg is lifted into a figure-four position and held by the ankle. The head tilts slightly to one side. Continue to develop from this hot button and the decision influencer will require more information with which to sell your proposals on to his bosses. The leg comes down and his stance is wide open, receptive. He leans forward and his hands do the rest, almost begging.

Here is a more aggressively negative decision influencer. His arms are tightly folded, his chin is down, his legs are stiff and his ankles are locked together. He is decidedly frosty. But hit a hot button and his chin will come up, his legs will pull back. He is more open but the ankles are still crossed, the arms still folded. Keep going and one arm will unfold and begin stroking his chin – a sure sign that he is interested. Stroking stops, head tilts to one side and he is ready to proceed. Go for it.

Here is a senior executive in the final throes of deciding to buy – he is leaning forward, eager. He stops stroking his chin and looks directly at the salesperson. Don't miss this one. He's waiting for you to ask for the order.

And for any dumb salespeople who have come this far and still feel that dreaded fear of having to ask creeping nearer . . . if you see this kind of impatient eagerness – palms of his hands rubbing up and down his thighs – ask for the order quickly but confidently.

'Can we call it a deal, then?'

'Will you sign up with us?'

'Can I have your order today?'

'How many do you want to stock for the first month?'

If you *don't* ask, this guy will throw you out on your ear.

BUILD YOURSELF A BENEFIT BANK

Every salesperson should develop a benefit bank, covering all the reasons a customer should buy and cross-referenced with the competition's benefits. It is vital to have a fund of reasons why the customer should buy from you.

You should be able to present the features and their resultant benefits in an easy, unambiguous way and demonstrate that your product or service is unique in some way or has a strong advantage which customers will not get from alternative suppliers. Once you have the benefits sorted out, then you just have to learn the best way to present them.

Remember, research has shown that there are five presentation words which really turn customers on. When they are used customers will sit up and listen. They will also remember them after you have left.

INCREASE

IMPROVE

REDUCE

SAVE

GAIN

Try to use all five, linking them into your benefit bank.

If you plan it right, you will find you are closing to the right person at the right time on the right product or service. If you use the win-win formula, you will find that the sales process will gather its own momentum, carrying itself through to a natural close. By making sure that the customer is 'ready' to be closed, the closing itself is almost a formality.

```
┌───────┐
│       │
│   6   │
│       │
└───────┘
```

For Sales Managers and Sales Directors Only . . . on Benefit Bank Development, Proofs and Selling Tools

(Salespeople should move directly to Chapter 7)

I want to ask all the sales managers and sales directors who are reading this book some serious questions. Do you give your salespeople the training and the tools they need to maximise their opportunities to close? Do you help them develop their benefit banks? Do you regularly update and refresh the data in those banks and test your salespeople on their competence in using the benefit bank?

Have you provided specific tools for converting negative responses into a positive response? For example, a customer says: 'Looks good. Send me a quote.' Is this serious or is it a put-off? Why do they want a quote? Do they need to sell the proposal to someone else who has the power to make the decision? Are they saying 'Send me a quote' because they haven't got the guts to say what they really want to say, which is, 'No. Go away and leave me alone'?

The benefit bank, the proofs, the selling tools, should all be dedicated to changing this very common 'Looks good. Send me a quote' into '*Looks great. When can we have it?*'

And for the staller who says, 'I need to wait for a few more quotes', the benefit bank, the proofs and the tools need to be dedicated to turning this into, '*This looks like the best deal I'm going to get.*'

And for that old, everyday chestnut 'I'll think about it', the benefit bank, the proofs and the tools need to be dedicated to achieving the response, '*Let's do it right away.*'

Without *your* help, very few of your salespeople will do anything about this on their own. Without *your* help, probably 75 per cent of their closing opportunities will go down the drain. You're paid to *do* something about this, so *do* it.

Start with the most powerful selling tools there are, and the easiest ones for you to acquire: letters from satisfied customers, third-party references, referrals in writing.

How many such letters are buried in the files, forgotten and never used? Dig them out. Send copies (at least ten of each) to every salesperson. Provide display albums so that they can use them professionally. Add at least six customer letters to every proposal and quotation you send out.

How many customer letters are in your salespeople's files, jealously guarded, for their eyes only? Who the hell do they think they're in competition with? Their own colleagues? Their own company? Get hold of those letters and circulate them to *every* salesperson.

A third-party reference letter doesn't have to be written directly to the person using it to be effective proof. *Any* letter to *any* person in your company that says 'We are very pleased with the service and would recommend it to anyone' is the most powerful closing tool you can get.

Set your salespeople a target and make things happen. Each salesperson *must* secure one new customer letter each month. No excuses. After six months you'll have enough good letters to build them into a special brochure – *What the Customers Say* – about your business. Produce a new brochure every six months, containing all the new letters, and in two years you will have eclipsed your competitors with this alone.

7

Overcoming Price-Conditioning

Many salespeople seem to be obsessed with price, much more so than most customers. Their obsession usually comes out in the form of offering discounts, which can become a drug to some salespeople. Just like drugs, discounts can screw you up.

If you offer 5 per cent discount this time, customers will ask for more next time, and the salesperson will have a hard time talking them out of it.

Prospective customers need to be conditioned about price. They are price-sensitive only as a result of the actions of the sales profession.

People use price to indicate the value of the product. If you are thinking of booking into an hotel for a weekend away but know nothing about the place, you would use the room price as an indication of the value of the product. If a second-hand car salesman welcomes you on to the forecourt with the announcement that this car 'has £200 off the screen price this week', you immediately know that he wants to sell you the car more than you want to buy it. If he is willing to give you that much off, then the chances are that you will ask for a bit more. You have been negatively price-conditioned. If, however, he works at selling the perfect vehicle to you, asking you questions about your needs and stimulating your interest and desire to buy, only talking about price at the end, you are then in a more positive frame of mind towards both him and the car. You have been positively price-conditioned.

If customers say, 'It's too expensive', never argue with them and never agree with them by offering to make a concession. Just ask, 'Relative to what?' Establish the facts they they are working with. Are they comparing it to the last time they bought this particular product or service? Are they comparing it to something completely different? Are they comparing it to their available budget or to the prices of the competition or to something they heard in the pub the other night?

Keep price-conditioning in mind all the time you are listening and talking. Prepare customers for the fact that if they want the best solution to their problem, they must expect to pay for it.

NEVER KNOCK THE COMPETITION

Never run down the competitor's products, but make sure that you know more about them than your customers do. Otherwise they could be running rings around you.

If your customers tell you that a competitor's price is 10 per cent lower than yours but they will do a deal if you can match it, they are telling you something very important. They are saying that they would prefer to buy from you. If they wanted to deal with the competition, they would want you to undercut in order to justify the risk. If they can buy it cheaper, why are they discussing it with you at all? Perhaps the competition can't make the delivery in time or produce sufficient quantities.

The customer has already agreed that they need the product. You now only have to 'sell' them on the extra 10 per cent cost – not a difficult task compared to selling the whole 100 per cent of the product. If they claim that yours is a more expensive product, you must know why that is. Is it because it is more reliable? Does it last longer? Is it made better? Is it easier to use? If they continually harp on about the cost, try asking them if they always buy on price. If the answer is 'Yes', then ask what sort of car they drive. If they admit to driving a Reliant Robin or a Skoda, then you are probably talking to the wrong person, but the chances are that they drive something a bit more expensive because of its comfort, power, reliability, service back-up or whatever.

JUSTIFY THE DIFFERENCE

People will always pay more for something if they feel they are getting more for their money, but they won't pay more for an identical product. If customers ask you how much discount you are willing to give, don't answer and don't haggle. Remember that, in the long term, the more you discount the harder it becomes to sell. If customers say they want a discount, never reply by asking how much they are looking for. You would be giving them a licence to knock you down.

THE RIGHT WAY TO CLOSE ON A DISCOUNT

If customers do ask for a discount, check that they are ready to make a buying decision there and then if the price can be agreed. If you can't do a deal today, don't give a discount. Otherwise they will use your price to shop around. Never give a discount to someone who isn't going to buy from you.

Don't feel you have to go up in 2·5 per cent jumps. Keep an open mind, but don't haggle like a market trader. That would devalue you and your product.

If customers say they can do the deal today, then turn it into a *trade*, not a *gift*. If you give a 10 per cent discount, will they pay cash on delivery? If you give a discount, will they buy a greater volume? If they agree to changes in the after-sales package, then perhaps you can drop the price. If they agree to a longer contract of commitment, then perhaps you can make a concession on the price.

Educate customers to realise that if they want something, they will have to give something. That way you are not devaluing the product.

THE ADDED-VALUE CLOSE

You can charge higher prices only if you are giving added value, but you have to make sure customers understand that.

Explain about all the things that they will gain by buying from you. You have to demonstrate all the benefits the higher price includes. Be brave enough to look customers in the eye and say: 'Part of what you get for this price is me.'

Then look at the minus side, and give examples of what would be taken away if they decide to buy something cheaper. Make some calculations, such as dividing the cost by the lifespan of the product. Rather than talking about a cost of £1,000, talk about £10 per week for the next two years. Then multiply the savings and gains which your product will offer, making the figure as high as possible. You are looking to make the costs look smaller and the savings look bigger.

You need to have all these figures at your fingertips before you go in for the close, but it will be more effective if you actually work them out in front of the customers, as if for the first time. If they agree the calculations with you as you go along, they will have to agree with the conclusions thrown up.

By adding value to the package you are offering, you minimise you own 'price fight' and weaken customers' price resistance.

THE SUICIDE CLOSE

This is a true story.

A replacement-window salesman called on a customer who was haggling about the price and driving a hard bargain. They talked for a while and finally the salesman said: 'OK, I'm not actually the salesman who should be servicing this area, I'm the sales manager. The reason *I'm* here is that the salesman committed suicide yesterday.' The customer, taken aback by this novel form of closing, gave his commiserations and then asked what this actually had to do with him. 'Well,' said the sales manager, 'because I don't have to pay the salesman his commission on the sale, I can offer it to you as a discount.'

The customer, who was actually one of Structured Training's course directors, laughed and said: 'That's the first time I've heard of the Suicide Close.' The sales manager thought for a moment and nodded. 'Right on. It's a cracker, ain't it!'

The customer did not buy.

THE JOHN RUSKIN CLOSE

Early on in the sale, ask customers if you can establish whether they believe in buying on price or on value for money. They will almost certainly go for value. Later on in the meeting take a business card out of your pocket with a quote from John Ruskin (1819–1900) on the back and point out that it is over 150 years old. Either give it to the customer or offer to read it out:

'It is unwise to pay too much, but it is unwise to pay too little. When you pay too much you lose a little money and that is all, but when you pay too little you sometimes lose everything, because the thing that you've bought isn't capable of doing the thing which it was bought to do.

The common law of business balance prohibits you from paying a little and receiving a lot – it can't be done. If you deal with the lowest bidder it would be as well to add something for the risk you run, and if you can do that you can afford to buy something better.'

LAWFUL PREY

Ruskin penned an even more powerful potential Price Close:

'There is hardly anything in the world today that some man cannot make just a little worse and sell just a little cheaper, and the people who buy on price alone are this man's lawful prey.'

At Structured Training Ltd I encountered many sales directors who still thought training at rock-bottom prices was the best money could buy. I used the Ruskin quotation on the back of my business cards and I never encountered a single person who was happy at the thought of being somebody else's lawful prey.

DON'T STATE IT, SELL IT

When customers ask how much the product costs, remember that you are a salesperson. Don't simply say, '£2,000, plus VAT, plus delivery, etc., etc.' Instead, sell them everything they are going to get for the price. Do all the arithmetic – the adding, subtracting, multiplying and dividing – that we talked about earlier in this chapter. In this way customers will end up being *positively price-conditioned*.

$$\boxed{8}$$

Closing with a Clipboard

Every salesperson needs a decent-sized, quality clipboard in order to close a sale. You simply can't close effectively with a little pocket book. You need something professional-looking on which to make your notes, draw your diagrams and keep your benefit lists for instant access.

When you first meet prospective customers, you should begin by swapping business cards. If they don't have one, that might sound a warning bell at the back of your mind. Could it be that they aren't decision makers at all? If they do have a card and they give you one, then you should clip it on your board in front of you, so that you never forget their name and so that you use it more often.

Before you start, ask their permission to take notes. They are unlikely to say 'No' and will be impressed by your professionalism.

Plan the contents of your clipboard to make sure you get everything right. It should have check lists of all the questions you need to ask as well as the benefits which you should be getting across, plus any facts, figures or third-party reference letters which you are likely to need as part of your sales pitch.

THE ORDER FORM CLOSE

We have already covered this close in some detail in Chapter 4. 64 per cent of all retail/staple/fcmg salespeople favour it, and it is vital that a clipboard is used throughout.

THE CRITERIA FOR ORDERING CLOSE

The Criteria for Ordering (CFO) Close is the industrial equivalent of the Order Form Close. Just like its retail counterpart, it starts at the very beginning of the sale and runs through to the very end. It forms the basis of the entire presentation and proposal.

Inside your clipboard you will have a pre-printed list of all the major plus points for the product or service and for yourselves as suppliers. A second list specifies what each plus point means for your customer and for you (see sample CFO opposite). So you say to the customer: 'Which of these criteria are important to you?'

If the list has been well thought out, the customer will answer, 'All of them', and by the time you get to the bottom of the list you will have large ticks against each relevant plus point. You then know exactly in which direction to drive your sales presentation. Everything you have to do, to prove and to demonstrate, is on the list, and you will have prepared every answer.

Once it is all done, the list is still there in your clipboard and you are able to refer to it as you move in for the close.

'Have we satisfied your criteria for ordering on all the points I've ticked, then?' you ask innocently.

'Er . . . yeess . . . I think so.'

'Fine. Can you give me an order number, then, so that we can get cracking?'

THE BEN FRANKLIN BALANCE SHEET

When you are up against strong competition the CFO Close becomes an advanced form of the Ben Franklin Balance Sheet. In its simple form this involves taking a plain sheet of paper, drawing a vertical line down the centre and writing two headings – 'for' and 'against' – at the top of each column.

This is a great method for helping poor decision makers to reach a

What criteria for ordering does this customer use?

Plus points	Customer's criteria
PRICE	best value for money.
DELIVERY	keeping promises, or able to help you out because you've left it until the last minute before placing the order.
QUALITY	meets your specifications – and KEEPS meeting them with no scrap.
SERVICE RESPONSE	quick and effective – no delays which cost you money in lost production.
COMPETENCE	The Technical and Commercial Department gets your orders right, sorts out the paperwork right, deals with 'returns' without hassle or delay.
RELIABILITY	of the product. Documented record of performance which proves longer life.
RUNNING COSTS	as low as possible.
MAINTENANCE COSTS	as low as possible.
PERFORMANCE	maximum possible on a consistent basis.
SAFETY	meets all the current and known future regulations – also will be acceptable to your workforce.
COMMUNICATIONS	easy to do business with. Easy to get hold of the people you want to talk to.
PHILOSOPHY	the company puts the customer first, not its own problems.

sion. The 'for' list, with your able assistance, should be three times as long as the 'against' list.

When it's a case of customers being unable to make up their minds between one supplier and another, the columns on your clipboard sheet should be headed with the names of the suppliers under consideration.

Your company's name should always be on the far left.

If you have a CFO list, *your* column should already be completed. Take it out from under the clip in your clipboard and slip it into a clear plastic pocket on the inside cover, so it's on the far left when your clipboard is open.

Your competitors get all the right-hand-sheet space, but with your CFO list on their left, how can they win? You never, never knock your competition; just point out the differences. 'Against' doesn't mean a bitching list.

And by the way, you *always* start with your list and never with the competition's, just in case customers are called away in the middle of your presentation. Imagine leaving them with a list of your competition's plus points only – and in your handwriting.

You can win in two ways. You highlight the plus points of your deal, which are over and above what the competition is offering according to the lists in your clipboard. You can also use these plus points to justify any price difference which is not in your favour. You then apply the 'options lost' technique, and go through your competitor's lists, highlighting what customers *won't* get if they buy from *them*.

'Well, it looks pretty obvious, doesn't it?' you conclude, and then close.

THE OPTIONS LOST CLOSE

The Options Lost Close is also a powerful tool when you're faced with customers who are telling you they're going to wait a while and think about it – and you know they're going to throw away a chunk of money if they do that.

You simply have to write down on your closing clipboard a list of the options they will lose if they don't buy *now*. Things like:

The special December campaign discount.

The price which goes up 8 per cent on 1 January.

Delivery before Christmas.

The loss of benefit for the month they're thinking it over.

The longer you can make this list the better. Then you add up all the items, having quantified them all in money terms, and you have a lump sum written down which customers can clearly see is the *cost* of their delaying the decision.

'That's a terrible waste of good money while you are worrying for a month or two,' you point out. 'Wouldn't you rather not have the worry?'

THE WEDDING-CAKE CLOSE

This is a natural follow-on to a comparison of your check list with an established supplier's. You've already proved that you have the edge and can provide a better all-round quality deal, but you still have to fight against years of entrenched habit.

'It would be unreasonable of me to expect you to give me *all* your widget business, and for you to discard old Snodgrass after all these years,' you say. 'It would be like a guest at a wedding reception eating the whole wedding-cake. I'm not greedy. But how about giving us a *slice* of the wedding-cake – 20 per cent, say, of your widget business? That way you keep Snodgrass happy, you try us out and, with two suppliers, you have second-source insurance, keeping both of us on our toes in the right kind of competitive spirit. You can't lose.'

And as you speak, you draw the wedding cake on your clipboard pad, with a small slice cut out of it. But practise first. Drawing cakes is not everyone's cup of tea.

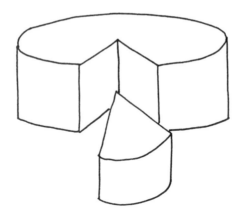

If the customer buys, then of course you go for a bit more of the business each time you call back. From 20 per cent to 50 per cent is an easy jump to make, unless you let someone down.

THE DIARY CLOSE

Instead of a clipboard use your diary. It could be a pocket diary, but a handsome desk one will be much more effective.

Get into the habit of carrying the diary with you in every selling situation. At the end of the sale, when you have covered everything except *when* the customer is going to get delivery, you get out the diary as you close, open it at the next month and say:

'Now, I want to be available for when the unit is delivered. I always like to make sure personally that everyone is happy on the first day. When would you *like* delivery? What's *your* most convenient date and time?'

Most customers will say, 'I'm not too bothered.'

'OK,' you say. 'If we said, er . . . Tuesday 15 December at 10.15 in the morning . . . how's that sound?'

'Sounds OK.'

'Great.'
You shut your diary, stand up and extend your hand.
'It's a pleasure having you as a customer.'

SIGNING-UP TECHNIQUES

If you are using an Order Form Close, all you have to do is turn the clipboard round, extend it towards the customer with a pen and say:
'Will you just OK this for me, then? Here at the bottom.'
With other sorts of close, you finish off with the One-Two Close:

1. Are you happy with everything?

2. Can we go ahead, then?

Once you have asked these two questions you really do have to shut up and endure the pressure of your own silence – for at least five seconds, and preferably more if the response is slow in coming.

X MARKS THE SPOT

This specific signing-up technique is useful in any kind of selling where you use an order form or credit finance document.

You fill the form out and then you put a pencilled X where the customer has to sign. You then hand the customer the form in your clipboard, which still has the Criteria for Ordering list clearly visible on the left-hand side. You don't need to say anything!

As soon as the form is in front of the customer, get up and check a measurement or something similar (go to the loo, perhaps) and if when you get back the form still isn't signed, offer your pen. If you can bear it, still don't say anything. Words might let the customer off the hook.

THE OBJECTIVES CHECK LIST

A particularly effective check list is one which covers the customer's objectives. (See the example opposite.)

The salesperson can actually use the list to broaden the mind of the prospective customer, opening up a whole new world of possible cost savings and productivity increases.

The list should be produced at an appropriately early stage in the presentation, with the salesperson explaining:

'Our products usually enable our customers to achieve seven objectives which are pretty important to them. Most of these involve saving money. I've got the objectives listed on this sheet. Can I just run through them and ask which of them are relevant to your situation?'

The salesperson runs through the list of objectives with the customer, who will almost certainly be actively worried about some of the items, though others might not have seemed relevant before. In most cases customers will agree that they want to achieve all seven of the objectives; they never want less than four of them.

Once their objectives have been identified, the salesperson goes on to define more precisely what the customer wants to achieve for each section. The precise objectives are written in the spaces provided under each heading.

The seller then asks the prospective customer to put the objectives in order of priority, after which the selling and the justification for the purchase should be plain sailing. The completed Objectives sheet becomes the first page of any resultant proposal.

OBJECTIVES

Customer _____

Date _____

What does the customer want to do – and why does he/she want to do it?

Detailed objectives that this customer wants to achieve (Strike out the sections which do not apply)	Order of Priority
INCREASE PRODUCTION/THROUGHPUT/VEHICLE TURNROUND	
REDUCE HANDLING TIME	
REDUCE LABOUR REQUIREMENT	
REDUCE MAINTENANCE COSTS	
BETTER UTILISATION OF EQUIPMENT	
BETTER UTILISATION OF SPACE	
IMPROVE LABOUR RELATIONS/SAFETY (Union attitude, accident rate, absenteeism, fatigue)	
OTHER FACTORS?	

9

For Sales Managers and Sales Directors Only . . . on Building Check Lists for the Closing Clipboard

(Salespeople should move directly to Chapter 10)

Well, here's some more work for you to do. Provide each of your salespeople with a good-quality, A4-size, professional-looking clipboard. Few of them will buy one for themselves.

Call a meeting of the entire sales team and get everyone's input into building a Criteria for Ordering list for each of your products or services and your customer's Objectives lists.

Take your salespeople through the practice of using them. Test their knowledge of your competitors. Make sure they each carry a *large* page-a-day diary. Make sure they can each draw wedding cakes.

Do all this, and look forward to a significant upturn in business.

10

Closing over the Telephone

Most salespeople seem to be terrified of the telephone, but it is in fact their greatest asset. It is one of the most powerful marketing tools available to salespeople, but only if they choose to use it effectively.

More excuses are given for failing to attain objectives via the telephone than in any other area of selling, whether it be appointment making, order taking or closing. Everyone sees the problems involved with the telephone but never the opportunities. It is vital to study your telephone technique in detail, then maximise the strengths and minimise the weaknesses.

Some salespeople seem to forget what the objective of their call is and simply end up having a nice friendly chat to the customer, with no positive outcome. This may be very pleasant, but it is not selling. Others attack every phone call in a high-pressure, results-orientated manner, ignoring the important aspect of selling themselves and not taking into account the emotional impact their voice is having on the customer. The result is that customers don't like what they are hearing and immediately put up barriers.

In between these two extremes is a successful balance of tangible and intangible elements.

THE TWIN-TRACK APPROACH

This can be one of the most effective tele-selling methods. It makes use of two tracks, the tangible and the intangible, to plan and execute calls.

The Intangible Track

1. Make sure you approach the telephone with a positive 'Yes, I can' attitude, because it will come across in your voice and you will infect the listener with your confidence.

2. *Smile* before you pick up the phone. It may sound corny, but it will make a difference to your voice. When the corners of your mouth turn up, your voice *always* comes out happy.

3. Use every opportunity to sell yourself and your company.

4. Seek out the maximum you can do for the customer, not the minimum. That doesn't just mean doing the maximum for the ones who shout the loudest.

5. Make sure that you *never* over-promise or under-deliver. Promises are like babies: they are fun to make, but sometimes very difficult to deliver.

6. Make sure you always sound polite, helpful and caring. Try listening to a recording of yourself to make sure you sound as you think you do. Putting personality and projection into your voice takes constant practice.

7. Remain alert to customers' moods and tones of voice, and then respond accordingly. Listening is a conscious mental process, whereas hearing is just a physical act.

8. Empathise with customers' concerns and needs, which means seeing their point of view without necessarily agreeing with it.

9. Always accept complaints as opportunities to improve your service, never as problems.

10. Ask yourself when a customer last said, 'Thanks for your help and advice.' It should be happening all the time.

The Tangible Track

1. Define your objectives, whether it is appointment making, research or making a final close. If you can't achieve your main objective, what will be your fall-back objective?

2. Always have all the relevant paperwork, records and your diary to hand when you call.

3. Make sure you have an effective and flexible word track, with all your key points ready.

4. Work out an effective attention getter to open up the conversation.

5. Prepare your key questions and make sure they are open and not closed. 'Yes' and 'No' answers over the phone are worse than useless.

6. Make sure you have your benefit bank complete and to hand. You are more likely to get an appointment if you talk benefits rather than features.

7. Listen for 'ready' signals, and be prepared to use a trial close the moment you hear one.

8. Prepare recovery routes which will bring you back on track from the objections which are likely to arise.

9. Promise yourself that you will attempt to close every call to the *highest* objective.

10. Keep a record of your conversion of calls to completed objectives, and check that your ratio is improving on a steady curve.

A recent analysis showed that 74 per cent of successful tele-closers use the Alternative Choice Close, just as in face-to-face selling.

At switchboard level the seller can ask:

'Would you be able to help me with some information that I need or would you prefer to pass me on to someone who can?'

At secretary level:

'Would it be possible for me to talk to Mr Jones now or would it be better if I called back later this afternoon?'

At customer level:

'If today is inconvenient how about me coming in to see you next Tuesday? Would the morning or the afternoon be better?'

If you offer customers a choice, they are likely to make one rather than simply say 'No'. By rejecting one of the alternatives they are, by inference, accepting the other.

TRIAL CLOSING

When you get a 'ready' signal, you can use a trial closer. It is much harder to spot the signals when you aren't face to face, but it can help to ask questions.

'Is week fifty important to you for this delivery schedule?'

And then listen. If the answer is, 'Yes, it is very important, we would have to have it during that week', then they are ready to be closed.

If you can tell that the customer is imagining owning the product, then you are practically there.

Customers will also use 'If we . . .' phrases on the phone.

'If we decide to go with you, could you install it for us?'

Don't just answer 'Yes'. Ask another question back:

'Absolutely no problem. When would you like us to do the installation?'

Be aware of changes in tone of voice. A laugh or chuckle suggests the customer is imagining owning the product.

The worst thing customers can say to you is, 'I'm not quite ready yet.' However, if you are prepared with your recovery routes, you can ask what points are still worrying them and go through things once more.

SELLING ACROSS

Always help customers obtain a complete package. If they are buying a product from you which needs something else to go with it (such as sand with cement, nails with a hammer), make sure that you can offer it to them somehow.

This is another way to use the twin-track approach. The telephone is an ideal method of adding on another product once the first sale has been made. Customers actually enjoy being sold across, because once they have made the first decision to purchase they are impatient to get the final result. If they have been sold a bag of cement it is because they want to see the wall built at the bottom of their garden. So they will be keen to buy the bricks and sand, and to hire a cement mixer and whatever other tools they need. And there is nothing as frustrating as buying a new toy for the children, taking it home and unwrapping it, only to find that there are no batteries. Why didn't they sell me some batteries?

SELLING UP

This means increasing the value of the sale and again, customers *enjoy* the experience. They will be very frustrated if they buy the first product you suggest, only to find a few months later that there is something else on the market which is just marginally more expensive but does a great deal more for them.

But, if you are going to add value to the sale by moving the customer to a product further up the market, don't do it simply to make a bit more money, because that does not create a win-win situation.

CLOSING ON A COMPLAINT

Angry customers are like balloons full of hot air. They are in a very volatile, potentially explosive state.

You could argue with them and concentrate on winning the argument rather than the sale. This is like sticking a pin in the balloon: you will find that you end up with no balloon and hence no customer.

You could disclaim responsibility, saying that it's not your problem, which is tantamount to just letting go. The air would come rushing out, but you would have no idea where the balloon would go. It might end up in your managing director's office, with the competition, or on a consumer watchdog programme.

As long as the balloon is still inflated there is a chance that the situation can be saved. The best way is to hold on firmly to the balloon, which means taking responsibility and letting the air out gradually, in a controlled way. This means listening to the complaint for as long as the customer wants to talk about it.

Whoever answers the telephone must take possession of the complaint. If it is you, from the moment you answer it is your problem. You *own* it. Once you have asked the questions and empathised with the customer, the air will go out of the balloon. You then say, 'This is what I propose to do about the problem.' If the customer says, 'Yes, I agree', then you have solved the problem and the sale can be saved. If the customer says, 'No', then you have to do some more questioning and some more listening because there is still some air in the balloon. When you are in full possession of the facts, you can start making suggestions:

'So that will sort out this month's stock holding for you, Mr Jones, and to make sure the same thing doesn't happen again, shall we increase next month's stock holding to 80 per cent of the range? Shall I just add it to the invoice, or would you prefer a separate one?'

If you pick your moment, you can close very successfully on a complaint. If you solve a problem for a customer you will be cementing a relationship, and they will come back to you again the next time they have a problem.

'FOLLOWING UP QUOTATION' CLOSES

To start with, it is better never to send quotations but to send 'proposals' instead.

Don't ring up saying, 'Have you received our quote?' You are merely asking for a negative reply. Instead, try saying, 'Last week we sent you our proposals for increasing/improving/reducing/saving/gaining . . .'

Don't say, 'Have you had a chance to read it through?' Try saying, 'Can you give me the go-ahead? We're all ready at this end.'

If customers say that they have a few queries or points they're not happy with, don't say: 'Oh, what are they?' That will get you into objection handling by telephone. Instead, say, 'Right, I'm back in your area next week. I'll come over and go through them with you. Which day is most convenient for you, Monday or Tuesday?'

EXPLODING THE MYTH

There is a piece of perceived wisdom (i.e. bullshit!) which says that it is impossible to get big decisions over the phone. Most salespeople and managers believe that it can't be done. But it can, if you believe it can. Adopt a 'Yes, I can' attitude.

An eighteen-year-old salesperson, fresh back from one of Structured Training's 'Selling by Telephone' courses, proved this by closing an order for £1·2 million over the telephone. She has subsequently closed many more deals this way, perhaps because she has been trained to know that it *is* possible.

Remember the bumble bee?

11

Classic Closes

Here is a mixed bag of the real-life classic closes which have, over the years, served to make their users rich. They can be adapted and used by anyone who has the determination and open-mindedness to be really successful in this great profession called selling.

WHEN IS AN ORDER REALLY LOST?

This is about an order which was won *after* the customer had placed the same order with a competitor and paid a deposit of £1,800. The product was a piece of metal finishing machinery – a kind of rumbling barrel with knobs on.

Our hero, the salesperson who found that he had lost the order to a competitor, reported this calamity to his sales director. The sale director said, 'Hang on a minute. We've got one of these in stock. We could deliver it to them tomorrow. What delivery is the competition offering on this?'

'Six weeks minimum,' replied the salesperson.

'So all is definitely not lost,' said the sales director. 'Come on, let's go and talk to the customer.'

So they sat down with the customer and worked out the figures, which showed that by saving the six weeks' delay on delivery they could save the customer three times the £1,800 he had paid as a deposit. The works manager who had actually placed the order was very reluctant to let down the company with whom he had made the deal, and didn't believe that his managing director would allow it. So they went to see the managing director and laid all the figures out in front of him. The managing director was also doubtful about doing this to the competing supplier, so the sales director offered a further discount of £1,800 over the first year on the chips that went into the machine, and the deal was done.

SO WHEN IS AN ORDER REALLY LOST? NEVER!

As an extra bonus, the competition made such a song and dance about losing the deal that the customer ended up banning them from his premises for ever.

THE 'PRICE IS HIGHER' CLOSE

This is for salespeople with guts and tremendous willpower. They also need to have a top-quality product or service.

It begins when the customer says to the salesperson: 'Your price is higher than the other people I've been talking to.' The salesperson nods, says seriously, '*Yes*, it is,' and then shuts up. After a few seconds the customer can't stand the silence and says, 'I suppose you'll say that's because yours is better?' And the salesperson nods again, says seriously, 'Yes, it is,' and shuts up again.

After a few seconds of this, most customers will sigh, say, 'OK, then' and buy.

THE 'PHONE THE BOSS' CLOSE

This is sometimes called the Executive Co-Operation Close.

This time our hero is dealing with a final objection. He *knows* it's a final objection because he's already asked, 'Is this the only thing that's standing in the way of us doing business?'

It's only a point on price or delivery that is holding things up, with the customer wanting delivery two days sooner or digging his toes in for a 2·5 per cent discount. The salesperson can't take these sorts of decisions, so he asks the customer if he can use the phone to call his boss. The customer, of course, says, 'Sure, go ahead.'

The salesperson rings his boss, explains the problem and gives the impression that he is having a hard time defending the customer's position. The boss gives in, apparently reluctantly.

The salesperson looks at the customer, with the phone still to his ear, and says, 'My boss says he'll do it, but only if I can give him an order *now*. Is that OK?'

Very rarely indeed is it *not* OK. So he tells his boss to go ahead and deliver, and the customer is impressed that the salesperson has pulled out all the stops for him.

THE COFFEE PERCOLATOR CLOSE

There are some up-market retail outlets which use this close very effectively when customers are on the premises.

When they come in, offer them a coffee and make sure that it is so hot that they can't possibly start to drink it for ten minutes. They consequently have to sit there talking to you or look around the stock, and they become *obligated* to buy *something*. You have, after all, extended a gesture of friendship and hospitality towards them.

The same principle also works well on small, under-staffed exhibition stands. One or two people can service a dozen prospective customers while they're waiting for their coffees to cool down to drinking temperature. It can even be a good idea to design the stand to look like a café, which will attract tired visitors to sit down for a rest and refreshment.

PUBLIC CLOSES

This means giving a presentation to a group of people, who may not all be from the same company, and closing the whole group. If you can get one or two of them to say 'Yes', the whole group will follow, rather like sheep.

I gave a demonstration of this technique live on television in 1983 (a time when high unemployment was a 'hot' issue). There was only one chance to get this right. The customers were forty members of the Cheltenham Townswomen's Guild, and the product was the all-British McLoud Dishwasher. It was more expensive than some of the competitors' products but very reliable.

I used three pre-close stages to get to the real close, and all forty prospects said 'Yes'. It went as follows:

Pre-Close 1

'How do you feel about unemployment? I read somewhere the other day that we're losing 20,000 jobs a month in our manufacturing industries.

'Terrible. But I also read that if everyone in the country spent another £3 a week on British goods instead of foreign goods, this 20,000 jobs a month loss would turn into a 60,000 jobs a month gain. It's staggering to think it could be that easy, isn't it?'

Pre-Close 2

'How do you feel about washing up?' (Muttered replies like 'horrible'.) 'How many hours a week do you spend doing it?' ('Too many.') 'Twenty perhaps? What could you do with that time if you didn't have to waste it washing up? How many of you have a dishwasher?' (Only one.) 'So all the rest of you do it the manual way.'

Pre-Close 3

'When you go shopping, especially when you're looking for something for the home that has to last a long time, do you look for the cheapest price or the best value for money?' (Unanimous 'best value'.)

The Real Close

'I would like to demonstrate to you a *British* product that's a bit more expensive than others you could buy, but it's very, very good – and if you like what you see, I'd like to arrange to do *another* demonstration in each of your homes, to make sure you can live happily with a dishwasher. How do you feel about that?' (Unanimous 'Yes'.)

THE CLIVE HOLMES COCKTAIL PARTY CLOSE

This is a classic from the king of the British life insurance industry. Clive Holmes is Life President of the Life Insurance Association, and a life member of the Million Dollar Round Table.

Very early in his career Clive discovered that if you tell a stranger at a cocktail party that you sell life insurance, the stranger disappears, almost like a puff of smoke. The words 'I sell life insurance' can clear a room faster than shouting 'Fire!' He went to a lot of cocktail parties because he knew that if he ran out of people to sell to, he was out of business. So he perfected a subtle change in his technique for his cocktail party prospecting which went like this:

STRANGER: What do you do for a living?

CLIVE: I buy life insurance.

STRANGER: (*Puzzled*) What do you mean, you buy life insurance?

CLIVE: I buy life insurance for people at the lowest possible cost for the maximum possible benefits. Would you like me to buy you some?

THE VICTOR HUGO CLOSE

This is another particularly good close for the pensions industry, using a quote from Victor Hugo: 'Nothing, not even prison bars, can hold a man as securely as poverty in old age.'

Like the John Ruskin Close discussed earlier, this is a great quote to have on the back of a business card, and can be adapted to fit most selling situations.

Any salesperson selling something which will increase the customer's profits can use the quote, just adding: '. . . and if your business doesn't increase its profits, you won't have much money to *put* into your pension fund, will you? Which, as you know, is the most tax-efficient thing a company owner can do with his money, Mr Jones.'

THE AUDIO CASSETTE CLOSE

This classic is about a salesperson who had submitted a proposal for a significant chunk of business to a customer he already knew reasonably well. But when he came to follow up the proposal, and secure the order, he found that his customer was never there when he telephoned or called in person. It wasn't evasion. The guy really was terribly busy, with responsibilities for three factories, each one fifty or sixty miles from the other. He was spending 80 per cent of his day in his car, and most of the other 20 per cent in the factories. His secretary saw him only for about ten minutes a week.

The salesperson knew that the customer was a Frank Sinatra fan, as he was himself. So he unearthed a very old, very rare 78 record of Sinatra that he was sure the customer didn't have. He copied the track on to a cassette and sent it to the customer through the post, with a suitable covering letter.

A few days later, the customer was in his car, burning up the miles towards one of his factories and playing the tape. After a few minutes of Sinatra, the music faded and he heard instead the salesperson's voice.

'Hi, Mr Arnold, I hope you like this tape. Sorry to interrupt, but I've been trying to speak to you for weeks now about our proposals for your chemicals supplies next period. If you have no queries, could you telex us the go ahead. Thanks. Enjoy the music.' And the music faded back in again.

The customer was so taken with the originality of the close, he phoned his secretary when he got to his destination and told her to send the telex.

CLOSING A CLOSED TENDER

There are, of course, many unethical ways to close a closed tender – what the Stock Exchange might call insider dealing and the law calls corruption. But there is also a perfectly ethical way of achieving the same end.

Most major closed tender deals take weeks or even months to reach tender stage. During those weeks or months, the suppliers who are being considered have numerous meetings with the customer's technical, commercial and financial people, to gather all the facts and figures so that they can tender meaningfully.

So this is what you do . . . After every meeting you send a report of the meeting's conclusions to every relevant customer contact. The report highlights the key benefits/cost savings that your deal will give the customer. By the time the tenders are in, there should be a dozen or more such reports in the customer's contact files. All or most of them stand a good chance of being paperclipped to your tender when it is examined. This is not a guarantee that you will win, but one company which has to give closed tenders regularly wins more than 50 per cent of the business it goes in for in this way – and at nowhere near the lowest price.

THE 'WE'VE A VAN IN YOUR AREA TOMORROW' CLOSE

This is an absurdly simple classic which has enabled one company in Berkshire to boost its sales turnover by 20 per cent in the first year that it started employing the close regularly.

Van deliveries are scheduled for the week ahead. The schedule is passed to someone in the sales office whose task it is to telephone every customer on the schedule the day before the scheduled delivery and say:

'You've got a delivery coming from us tomorrow. Is there anything else you'd like us to put on the van for you?'

Then that person calls up on the computer terminal all the other customers in the same town or on the route the delivery van will be taking and telephones them:

'We've a van coming your way tomorrow. Is there anything we can put on it for you?'

It seems so obvious, doesn't it? But we know from experience that what this company is doing is exceptional. Too many companies have systems which are not flexible enough to *allow* for a fast turn-around, or else their sales offices think it would be too much trouble. Many simply haven't thought about it – or believe it is too simple to bother about. One company executive actually said to me:

'It's not very sophisticated, is it?'

But an increase of 20 per cent in sales is a pretty sophisticated result.

12

Closing a Board of Directors

The boardroom can be a battlefield for salespeople, and in order to win any battle you need confidence. But that is the one thing that can drain out of any salesperson when confronted by a high-powered board of directors.

There are two battles going on in most of these situations, and neither of them is between the salesperson and the customers, because that sort of battle can lead only to a win-lose situation.

The first battle is happening within the salesperson's mind. When you lack confidence it means that there is a conflict going on inside your brain, the rational side fighting with the abstract side. That leads to an increased flow of adrenalin to keep the blood pumping around the body fast, so that you can run away from the problem. Successful salespeople, however, can never run away, not if they want to close the sale, but that doesn't make them any less nervous.

To win the battle of the nerves, you have to face up truthfully to what you are feeling. If you tell yourself you are feeling 'nervous' about the situation, you are actually using a euphemism for 'scared'. You must come to terms with how you feel and then you can deal with it. The way to achieve confidence is simply to know more about the subject than the people who sit around the boardroom table. If you are sure that you know more, your confidence will soar.

The second battle is between the board members themselves. Whenever you have a team of ambitious, intelligent, opinionated people, you will have differences of opinion and conflicts of interest. Some directors will be interested in maintaining the status quo, while others will be intent on changing it. Some will want what you are proposing, while others will be dead set against it. Your proposals are a theatre of war for these people.

At one company a new director was taken into the boardroom for the first time and shown the table. The man showing him around told him about a recently elected Labour politician going into the House of Commons for the first time and sitting down on the benches with the man who was showing him around. Looking across at the other side, the new MP said: 'So, that's the enemy, is it?'

'No, no,' said the old hand, 'that's the Government. This is the enemy here.'

That's the problem which most people face in the average boardroom. To overcome this problem you need to know what is motivating everyone, and to understand some of the basics of human behaviour and personality.

THE BEHAVIOURAL MIX

Everyone is made up of a unique behavioural mix. Personality characteristics are particularly noticeable around any boardroom table. Here are four examples:

The Customer with a Strong Need for Domination

This sort of customer tends to be abrasive and defiant in their behaviour. They may brag a lot and drop names more often than is necessary. They will try to monopolise any discussion and will be impatient with other people, interrupting them when they try to argue or put alternative points of view. They are argumentative and probably see no need for salespeople to exist at all. They will always claim to have all the answers.

A typical 'Domination' director once said that he didn't see why his company needed a salesforce; he saw salespeople as being a 'carbuncle on the backside of industry'.

How to deal with 'Domination' Customers

1. Never try to confront them. If you meet aggression with aggression you will just have conflict.

2. Control them passively by using open questions. Give them the impression that they are controlling the meeting.

3. Give them plenty of back-up data because you will need to cross every 't' and dot every 'i'.

4. Let them drive the sale for you.

5. Leave it to the other directors to shut them up.

The Customer with a Strong Need for Security

These people work on the premise that they had better keep their mouth shut so that their colleagues won't think they are stupid.

The stance here is silent and defensive. They will shrink back and say little, and will be very reluctant to come to a decision. They hate risk and want to maintain the status quo wherever possible. They are procrastinators and take a 'that won't work' attitude to everything.

One 'Security' director was heard agonising over a decision and saying, 'No, we made a wrong decision on something like this in 1958, and in 1964, and I'm not going to go through it again.'

They were talking about buying a coffee machine.

How to Deal with 'Security' Customers

1. Listen patiently and use open questions. You will need to watch their body language because they won't be saying much.

2. Do progress checks to ensure that you are talking on the same wavelength, and look for ways to become more tuned in to theirs.

3. Make the running with suggestions.

4. Prove that you have a good, reliable track record for both product and company.

The Customer with a Strong Need for Popularity

These people want to be liked first and to be effective second. That means they will always be friendly and agree readily with everything you say. It will be only a superficial agreement, however. They roam from topic to topic and they avoid conflict with poor-quality compromises.

A 'Popularity' managing director once said that he had a problem with a particular person in his team who hadn't achieved a single financial target or stuck to the business plan. Instead of firing him, however, he promoted him to 'Head of Special Projects'.

How to deal with 'Popularity' Customers

1. Be positive.

2. Stress optimism.

3. Use closed questions to discourage them from talking too much.

4. Don't focus on this person unless you have to.

5. Use this person as a supporter for your proposals.

The Customer with a Strong Need for Self-Realisation

These people take a pragmatic, flexible approach. They are solution-minded people. They tend to be self-assured but not arrogant. They are usually candid and open and will look for themes. They will not labour points and will take risks if they feel the returns are worth it. They are happy to be proved wrong and see differing opinions as constructive. They like constructive argument. They don't suffer fools gladly and, sadly, they are the customers that most salespersons like least, because they are very demanding and will test salespeople's beliefs. If a salesperson says something to them, they may well look him or her in the eye and say, 'Do you really believe that?' They are looking for conviction not sales-speak.

How to Deal with 'Self-Realisation' Customers

1. Stick to the point.

2. Be factual; don't use sales-speak.

3. Express conviction.

4. Welcome pertinent questions.

The 'Self-Realisation' customer is flexible and pragmatic, and that is precisely the sort of behaviour which good salespeople should adopt. They should be solution-minded and results-orientated.

Success in the boardroom, as in any selling situation, comes from preparation and planning and understanding what makes your customers tick.

HOW TO CONTROL THE MEETING

When facing a board of directors, you need to remain in control of the meeting, which means laying plans. The secretary to the managing director or chief executive will always be a key player in these plans. This person takes the minutes, sets out the agenda and keeps in touch with everyone. They are a gold mine of information and make a useful ally. They know who reports to whom and who has responsibilities for different parts of the project, and they will know which director puts the final signature on the order form. The salesperson needs to know which directors have a central interest in the purchase and which have only a marginal interest. This is all information which the secretary can tell you.

Make sure that you have a copy of the agenda and a list of the attendees before the meeting, and find out if the meeting has been called specifically to discuss your proposal and, if not, what its purpose is. Find out how much time you are going to have, and what questions they are likely to ask you. Enquire whether they would like you to take some technical support with you to field difficult questions, and then do all the research you can on the company itself, with annual reports for the previous few years and anything else you can lay your hands on.

Build up a profile of each director who will be there, knowing what their job history is, what their particular specialisation is and where they fit into the decision-making unit. Are they there to evaluate or to decide?

Finally, you need to know what competition you are up against and what benefits there are for the directors in saying 'Yes' to your proposition or to another one.

Some decisions taken in a boardroom have only a marginal effect on the customer company, while others have a major effect. So you need to build a benefit bank for each director, relevant to his or her needs. You need to ascertain whether the decision is going to change the balance of power around the table.

Remember, the more research you do, the more control you will have.

Seating

You can win or lose control of the meeting by being in the right or wrong seat. Never sit in the chairman's seat. Look for somewhere neutral to sit, somewhere half-way down the table. Sit as far as possible from the 'Popularity' person, because they have least credibility, and as near as possible to the 'Self-Realisation' person, because they have the most credibility, and you want to gain credibility by association.

Use of Names

The use of names will also help you to gain control. Draw up a seating plan with everyone's name on which you can refer to as you go along. The only reason not to use people's names is because you have forgotten them.

Introduce yourself properly and professionally.

With names you can control the conversation, calling people in or shutting them out. 'OK, Mr Jones,' you can say, 'can I direct this question particularly at you? How many people are currently tied up in this project?'

FLIP CHARTS

Flip chart presentations are another useful way of putting over your message. Make sure the flip chart is set up beforehand, and link it to the seating plan if possible.

Never show what you are going to talk about until you reach the relevant point in the presentation, otherwise you will take away any dramatic impact and give them time to mull over certain points out of context. Have 90 per cent of the chart prepared beforehand, so that your performance is already rehearsed, and 10 per cent to be filled in 'live' to give drama and relevance to the presentation, and to make it personal to the people in the room that day. You can outline lightly in pencil beforehand the things that you going to fill in on the flip chart in front of them.

THE QUALITY CLOSE

Senior decision makers are always interested in justification, so list on your flip chart all the reasons why they should buy from you, tailoring the reasons to each person around the table: the proposals to the production director will show how you will help production; the proposals to the finance director will show how you will cut costs; other directors will be interested in your added-value benefits.

You are selling the 'quality' of your company, its track record and commitment. You use whatever references you can to give these senior decision makers a watertight case for why they should use you.

CLOSING WITH FIGURES

You can achieve great things with figures, so why not use them to make your case . . . on your flip chart.

Don't use industry norm figures, averages or mean ratios unless you have to. Try to use the customer's own figures, because then the members of the board can't argue with them.

The best way is to develop the figures during your presentation to the board, as you go along. For example, ask the members of the board how many people are involved, and what the investment is and how many machines and so forth. Build these figures into a clear-cut case for their decision to buy. Work out the payback and the return of investment and cost benefits.

Often you will find that they are astounded because you have done something with their figures which they had never thought of doing before.

If they can't produce the figures you need, then have the industry norms in your bag, just in case. They are much better than no figures at all.

Concentrate on the costs, not the price, and look for angles like release of capital, reduction in wastage, projected production increases and anything which is likely to be a concern of the board.

Remember, numbers not words: you can only *read* words.

THE BIG-GUN CLOSE

The big gun in this case means a senior member of your management team, rather than a sawn-off shotgun (although there may be times when you feel the latter could be your only hope of closing a particularly stubborn member of a board!).

It might be helpful to take your own managing director along to the board meeting with you. It could help you to control the meeting and might also extend its remit, with the chairman of the customer company deciding he will attend where he might not have bothered had it just been a salesperson making the presentation.

Again, you will be gaining credibility by association. Some salespeople, due to lack of age or experience, find it difficult to sound authoritative to a group of senior people.

A salesperson with the support of his or her manager can ring the customer contact and say, 'I know you don't want me to attend this meeting, but I've mentioned it to my managing director, and they would very much like to come, and they say that they've got some cards up their sleeve which I know nothing about.'

But don't ever let your *ego* take over. Have the confidence to ask for this big-gun help!

USING THE BOARDROOM MOLE

The mole isn't exactly a spy feeding you information, but someone around the boardroom table who is your contact. They will probably be a decision influencer rather than a decision maker. You need to develop this person, keep in contact with them and give them all the help you can. They will help you to sell at the meeting which you cannot get invited to yourself.

The best moles are the 'Security' customers, the silent ones, because when they say something on your behalf everyone will listen. 'Popularity' people are the worst, because they are always rabbiting on.

If you can't get into the meeting, offer to give up the time to sit in their reception area, or on the end of the phone, in order to answer any questions that might come up. Very often your contact will come out and actually ask you about the competition.

The boardroom mole, therefore, is helping you to give feedback to a meeting even when you are not there.

THE LONG-WALK CLOSE

Often the chairman of a board meeting will want to kick the salesperson out of the room as soon as they have finished their presentation, so that the board can talk things over.

Anticipate this by going of your own accord. Once you are sure they have no more questions, volunteer to go to the toilet for a few minutes while they talk things over and tell them you will then be back to answer any questions they might have. They then have to talk about the proposal on the spot and come up with something concrete to ask, or else they have to give you the order.

If you are able to walk out of the room without being stopped, you will more than likely close that sale, but it is a very long walk from the table to the door.

Never turn round to look at them as you go.

13

What To Do *After* You've Closed the Sale

What else is there to say about closing the sale? You've won the order, the piece of paper is signed and in your bag. You are *safe* – or could you still mess it up?

Alternatively, could you actually achieve even more success from the situation? Could you turn this one successful order into three more?

There are a number of strict 'don'ts' in this post-close situation:

Don't accept a cup of tea or coffee.

Don't keep talking about the deal – in case you talk yourself back out of it.

Don't drop your guard.

Don't talk about politics, women, religion, the weather, money, sport, cars, other people, your competitors or their competitors . . .

So what on earth *do* you talk about?

If customers are pushed for time, take advantage of the fact. Be concerned for them and leave – fast.

If, however, customers are obviously *not* pushed for time, if they are relaxed and happy now that the big decision has been taken and all their anxieties have disappeared, then you can go *fishing*.

First you must bait your hook.

'Before I go,' you say casually, 'I wonder if you'd do me a great favour? One of my ever-present tasks is finding people who could use this kind of equipment (or service). Do you know anyone else who might have a need?'

Or you could start fishing by asking:

'If you and I swapped jobs tomorrow, who'd be the first person you'd call on?'

Everybody likes to be helpful and to tell other people how they would do their job, so all you have to do is take out five blank customer record cards from your briefcase, a pen from your pocket and get yourself poised to write.

As the customer spouts names, write them down, checking that you get the spellings right wherever possible, or at least enough information so that you can look them up in the phone book when you get back to the office. Try to get job titles and as much information about the sort of equipment or services these people are using at the moment.

You might get only one or two names before the customer either dries up or seems to lose interest in the game. Obviously you can't push people any further than they want to go. You could try one more question, such as:

'Has anyone you know gained promotion recently, gone up in the world or taken on new responsibilities?'

Or:

'Are you a member of any trade association or professional body?'

If the answer to the last question is 'Yes', then see if they can remember meeting anyone who might be interested in your products. You might ask them about their hobbies, and if, say, they play golf, whether they have met anyone down at the club recently who might be a potential customer.

If you approach this fishing technique correctly, you should be able to fill at least three cards, but ensure that you bring out five, because otherwise you'll never complete three. Why? Because very few customers will stop helping you until they have completed *half* your cards. It's a kind of mental compromise. And half-way to five is three. If you used three cards, most times you'd get only two of them filled in. But don't *stop* at three. Quite often you can get all five, sometimes even more. So have some spares in your briefcase.

Before your first card is fully completed you need the prospective customer's telephone number. Your existing customer may take a diary out of their jacket pocket to give you this. If so, watch what happens to the diary *after* you've been given the number. If it stays on the desk, the chances are you might be able to get some more names.

Finally, lay the cards out on the table and look at them. Select the one you feel is the best prospect. Pick it up.

'Er, you said you knew George Riley well . . .'

'Yes.'

'I couldn't ask you an enormous favour, could I? Would you give him a ring yourself for me, and ask if he has got time to see me today while I'm in the area?'

If you do it right, and it does take practice, most of the customers will make the phone calls for you as well. After they've put the phone down on the second you could say, 'Buy you a good lunch if you ring the other three.'

If business results from any of these calls, you go back and tell your customer, thank them properly and then in three months' time you might be able to go back for more names. If you master the fishing technique, you stand a chance of making three more successful sales from every one you make.

And you can even turn an unsuccessful close into several successful ones. If a customer gives you the 'I'd like to think about it' line, then you should be able to apply what is undoubtedly one of the greatest closes ever developed.

There is a replacement-window and patio doors company in the Midlands which is well known for its quality and service. Here this great close is known as:

THE 'YOU'RE PULLING MY LEG' CLOSE

The company's salespeople go through their usual presentation, complete with samples, third-party references, photographs, measurements and price calculations. If the customer still can't make up their mind, the salesperson gives a sigh of resignation and says:

'OK, but it would be a great deal for you and your wife. The value of the house would increase a lot more than the windows are going to cost. Anyway, I've done my best. Is there any chance you could help me before I go?'

Prospective customers relax. They feel they have been let off the hook now the salesperson has said they are going. They feel sufficiently guilty about messing them around to want to make some sort of amends.

'Sure,' they say, 'what can I do for you?'

'Do you know of anyone else around here who needs replacement windows, double glazing or patio doors?'

'Well, you could try Mr and Mrs Smith at Number 35. They've been talking about getting a new front door for months . . .'

Before you know it the customer will be chatting away about all sorts of people who are improving their houses. The salesperson should get three or four really good referrals. They make notes, check on names, addresses and needs, and ask if they can use the prospective customer's name as an introduction. Finally, they stop talking, look down at their notes for a few seconds, laugh and look back at the prospective customer.

'You're pulling my leg,' they tell the customer.

'What do you mean?' the customer replies, puzzled.

'You've got to be pulling my leg. You've given me four good referrals – people you know – and you aren't going to be buying anything yourselves. You've got to be pulling my leg. Come on, what's the real problem. Do you want to go over the finance figures again?'

Eight out of ten will withdraw their stall and will buy!

This technique could work in any selling situation. It is so powerful it is a target achiever on its own.

GOLDEN RULES

Without closing techniques your chances of making a successful sale are less than 20 per cent.

Remember, if you don't close, you're working for the competition.

Get into the habit of closing, and PRACTISE, PRACTISE, PRACTISE.

The best way to practise is to ask for an order on every call.

It doesn't necessarily have to be *the* order, as long as it is *an* order.

Promise yourself that you will never let a single piece of business be lost because you *didn't ask for it*.

So here's my closing question for you: 'Will you do it?'

Index

The Mercury titles on the pages that follow may also be of interest. All Mercury books are available from booksellers or, in case of difficulty, from:

Mercury Books
W.H. Allen & Co. Plc
Sekforde House
175–9 St John Street
London EC1V 4LL

Further details and the complete catalogue of Mercury business books are also available from the above address.

Michael Beer

The Joy of Selling

Countless thousands of people have at one time or another considered entering the selling profession. They have been attracted
by the idea of working with people, of dealing with fascinating
products, of the interesting life-style of the modern salesperson –
or simply by the potential for an income much higher than they
enjoy now.

Unhappily, most of these people don't ever get into selling.
There are too many questions which they need to ask and which
nobody seems to be able to answer:

Could I really succeed in selling?

What sort of selling is best for me?

How do I go about getting a selling job?

And, after all that:

How do I learn to sell successfully?

You will find the answers to these questions (and dozens of
others) in this book. Every detail is here to help you, from the
moment you decide to go for it to the first time you sit down in
front of a potential customer and make him yours.

Reading this book could be the most important step you have
ever taken.

*'There is a chronic shortage of good salespeople – a shortage which has been
getting steadily worse for many years. This book should make a major contri-
bution to reducing this shortage and make thousands of people richer and
happier.'* John Fenton

ISBN 1 85252 024 8 (paperback)

Jeremy Thorn

The First-Time Sales Manager

Sales managers are trained not born. This book is designed to meet that training need. Written for those about to take on new responsibilities, perhaps as their first major career step, it will also help existing managers who seek to extend their role and performance. Packed with practical tips, advice and examples, *The First-Time Sales Manager* deals with:

- *Managing – not selling*: the differences between sales management and selling; how to deal with bosses, colleagues and staff; the sales office and administration; statistics, computers and sales planning.
- *What a sales manager does*, and how to do it well: interviewing, recruitment and training; leadership, reward and motivation; field visits and appraisals; sales controls, reports and records; sales strategy and organisation; monitoring competitors and market trends; forecasting and business planning.
- *Marketing and strategic direction*: an introduction to basic marketing principles, including product development, planning and positioning; market segmentation and pricing strategy; packaging and promotion; advertising and exhibitions; distribution channels and competitor strategy.
- *How to handle problems*: what to do when someone leaves; how to handle difficult personalities on your team and ethical problems arising from dishonesty, illegality or dismissal; what to do when your team starts to miss its targets; competition and how to respond; sales meetings and conferences; you and your own career development.

Fully supported with check sheets, working documents and useful exercises.

ISBN 1 85252 050 7 (paperback)